"Ed Welch is a treasured friend. Every time I am with him I feel encouraged, listened to, challenged, and understood. This book does the same thing. He not only helps us deal with the major issues of life, but Ed brings Scripture alive to help us experience God's best for our lives."

> **Jim Burns**, Ph.D., President, HomeWord Center for Youth and Family; author of *Teenology* and *The Purity Code*

"In *What Do You Think of Me?*, Ed Welch carefully, surgically, exposes people-pleasing for what it is. He lets it be ugly—all sin is ugly!—and offers a much more satisfying vision rooted in the finished work of Jesus Christ. Whether you are young or old (but especially if you are young), you would do well to give this book a read."

> **Tim Challies**, Author of *The Next Story* and *The Discipline of Spiritual Discernment*

"As I read *What Do You Think of Me? Why Do I Care?*, I realized that it's all about eyes. In a riveting, real-life, raw way, Ed Welch provides a spiritual eye exam. In language that captures the heart and soul of every human being who ever longed to be known and accepted, Ed shows us what's normal, yet wrong, about our constant fear of the eyes of others. Then he gently, yet firmly, directs our gaze toward Jesus: all eyes on Jesus. That is the way of change. Finally, Ed points our focus onto others: they are our family who God equips us to love sacrificially. If you find that you're always living squinty-eyed, focused only on what others think of you, then read Ed's spiritual eye chart to see with clarity answers to your deepest questions about life and relationships."

> **Robert W. Kellemen**, Ph.D., Executive Director, Biblical Counseling Coalition; author of *God's Healing for Life's Losses*

"The sin that so easily entangles us all—living in light of what other people think of us. Ed Welch's brilliant insights into this unavoidable struggle are exposed at a level that makes him a skillful surgeon of the heart. Welch invites us to re-examine the crux of the issue with a profound theology that is uniquely practical, informative, and gospel-centered. Working on the college campus where students live to impress other people, this book is now where I will turn to help pastor them through this struggle and embrace the fullness of the gospel that Welch so eloquently flushes out for us."

> **Alex Watlington**, Reformed University Fellowship (RUF) campus pastor at Penn State University

WHAT DO YOU THINK OF ME? WHY DO I CARE?

Answers to the Big Questions of Life

Edward T. Welch

New Growth Press

www.newgrowthpress.com

New Growth Press, Greensboro, NC 27404
Copyright © 2011 by Edward T. Welch. All rights reserved.
Published 2011.

Cover Design: Faceoutbooks, faceoutbooks.com

Typesetting: Lisa Parnell, lparnell.com

ISBN 13: 978-1-935273-86-8
ISBN 10: 1-935273-86-8

Library of Congress Cataloging-in-Publication Data

Welch, Edward T., 1953–
    What do you think of me? why do I care? : answers to the big questions of life /
    Edward T. Welch.
        p. cm.
    Includes bibliographical references and index.
    ISBN-13: 978-1-935273-86-8 (alk. paper)
    ISBN-10: 1-935273-86-8 (alk. paper)
    1. Self-perception—Religious aspects—Christianity. 2. Theological anthropol-
ogy—Christianity 3. Youth—Religious life. 4. God (Christianity) I. Title.
    BV4598.25.W45 2011
    248.4—dc23
                                                                    2011029444

Printed in the United States of America

20 19 18 17 16 15 14 13   7 8 9 10 11

To Angelo and Barbara Juliani
Enduring friendships are a great gift.

Contents

Introduction

A confession. I still care what other people think about me. A critical email or letter can get me down (though I honestly want you to offer critical comments about the book if you have any). When I feel like a failure, and at times there are good reasons for me to feel that way, I notice my instincts to either boast or hide. But—and this is an important but—I know what to do. I know where to turn. More and more I find these down times to be opportunities to grow, and I think I am growing.

My experience with my own problems is that a personal problem is one thing; the hopelessness that can attach to it makes it much harder. By hopelessness I mean that it seems like nothing can be done about the problem. Take any problem you might have, subtract your hopelessness, add a hefty portion of hope, and guaranteed, things will look very different. So I can promise you that you will, at least, find hope in what is ahead.

This book sounds some of the same themes of an earlier book, *When People Are Big and God Is Small*. After I wrote that book, I kept working with this material, and now seemed like an appropriate time to jot down some of that progress. In another twenty years, maybe I'll do it again.

As I wrote the book I was thinking about people I know who are roughly between the ages of fifteen and twenty-five. You don't have to be in this age span to read it. I have profited from writing and reading this book, and I am much older than twenty-five. But the book would sound a little different if I were writing to a fifty-year-old. I would probably write more about sagging stomachs, wrinkles, and divorces than teenage girls who decide to be vampires.

It is a great topic. There is nothing superficial about it. What you will find is that it goes directly to the critical questions of life, which means that the direction set out here can guide you through lots of other problems too. I hope that it provokes you, inspires you, guides you, gives you hope, and is just plain enjoyable.

The Problem
The Heart of the Matter
Who Is God?
Who Am I?
Who Are They?

The Problem

This will be a brief walk through a common problem. In order to make it worthwhile, your first task will be to find the problem in yourself. The problem—which will be labeled as the fear of others' opinions—shouldn't be difficult to identify because it is something you and every person in history has had to manage, tolerate, and struggle with. Once you find it, you will learn what to do with it, which should actually be enjoyable.

As you read, go ahead and mark up the pages with your questions, answers, and reactions. It will make it seem more like a conversation.

1

Somebody Is Watching

"Lord, please let me be normal."

Okay, maybe you never actually prayed that, but you *do* want it. You want to fit in. Who doesn't? Imagine you are invited to a formal dinner, but you didn't read the entire invitation and you go in shorts and flip-flops. (Yes, it wasn't pretty. I was also wearing a Killer Dana T-shirt—it's the name of a surf shop, but the other dinner guests thought I was going gangsta.)

We all have these stories. We spend a lot of time concerned about fitting in, which means that we spend a lot of time thinking about our hair, our body, our intelligence, and our clothes so we can be part of the larger group. None of us want to be stared at if it means that the people looking at us don't like what they see. When they look at us that way we want to run and hide.

Oh, and there is another prayer too. "Lord, please *don't* let me be normal." "If I can't fit in, then I'll be a vampire," and she did just that. She figured that both fitting in and standing out were impossible, so she made a choice. Her parents would have preferred a more traditional route such as starting on the basketball team or high SAT scores. They are hoping it is a phase, which it is—there are not many fifty-year-old vampires. But, unless she discovers something else to run her life, she will always be looking for ways to stand out, and she will be depressed.

We want to stand out from the crowd. We want to be seen, which means that we want people to notice us and be impressed with something. We want them to respect us, to like us, and to love us. Not too many people dream of being average. Take a look at your fantasies, and you will probably find a quest to be noticed.

- Have you ever imagined that you scored the winning basket in the NBA finals?
- Do you enjoy superhero movies because you like to imagine what it would be like to have such powers?
- Do you identify with a celebrity because you would like to live her life, at least for a year or two?
- Have you ever fantasized that you were famous or great?
- Or maybe you have already given up on greatness and will settle for a B+.

It's complicated, isn't it? If only we could be less controlled by the opinions of others. Maybe a deserted island could be the answer. That would be a pricey way to avoid the judgments of others, but it might work. Apart from that option, you have a creepy sense that people are watching, judging, evaluating, accepting, or rejecting you. Sometimes the eyes belong to no one in particular. Other times you know exactly who or what group you are trying to please. Either way, you are controlled by other people more than you think, and other people, of course, are controlled by how you see them.

The problem is a common one, but we don't talk about it too often. As a way to get it out into the open, keep trying to locate this in your own life.

- Do you buy clothes because of what other people will think? Have you ever not gone somewhere because you didn't have the right clothes or didn't like the way you looked?

- Do you spend a lot of time in front of the mirror?
- Do you avoid people, either because you are angry with them or because you would be embarrassed if they saw you?
- Do you ever get embarrassed to be seen with your parents?
- Have you ever been embarrassed at the thought of other people knowing that you go to church?
- Have you ever been embarrassed to say you believe in God?
- Have you ever been embarrassed to say you believe in Jesus?
- Do you ever exaggerate to make yourself look better?
- Do you feel like a failure sometimes? Do you hate school because from the moment you walk in you feel like a failure?
- Are you afraid to ask questions in class because you might look stupid?
- Do you wish you were thinner, stronger, taller, shorter, smarter, faster, or better looking?
- Have you ever been jealous of someone thinner, stronger, taller, shorter, smarter, faster, or better looking?
- Have you ever wished you could shrivel up and disappear?

Agreed, these questions are too easy. You might hesitate on one or two of them, but basically the answer is yes across the board, and they are that way for everyone. They all point to how we can be too controlled by the opinions of others. Why do you think everyone struggles with it? Where does it come from? *Its part of our sinful oess and fear of man*

One of the riskiest things in life is to like someone—*really* like someone. It all starts innocently. You find yourself attracted to another person. Happens all the time. No big deal. But then the attraction grows, and amid the glow of romantic feelings lurks a monster:

what if you like the other person more than the other person likes you? *What will he or she think about me?* you wonder.

You send some friends out on a reconnaissance mission. Their job is to find out if the other person likes you *without* that person knowing your intentions. If word comes back yes, you can move toward that person safely. If the answer is no, you lick your wounds, thankful for the heads-up that saved you from total embarrassment. In your everyday life, the potential for rejection is enormous. It's amazing that so many people actually get out of bed in the morning. Sound familiar?

Success can't protect you. Steven King, the ridiculously prolific and famous horror writer, was told by Miss Hisler, his school principal, "What I don't understand, Stevie, is why you write junk like this in the first place." At the time, he was already writing scary stories that other students were willing to pay to read. "I was ashamed," he says of the incident. "I have spent a good many years since—too many, I think—being ashamed about what I write."* You too have probably heard words like Miss Hisler's, and they are still etched inside your soul. Can you think of some? Why do I like that? What does that mean?

Look around a little more and you will see it—it goes by many names: a desire for acceptance, the fear of rejection, painful self-consciousness, or peer pressure. You can see it when you or any of your friends take muscle-enhancing steroids or illegal drugs. You see it in anorexia, bulimia, and depression. You find it in people who are sexually active before or outside of marriage.

- What will they think of me?
- What might they think about me?

---

* Stephen King, *On Writing: A Memoir of the Craft* (New York: Scribner, 2000), 49–50.

- How can I be accepted?
- How can I be loved?

The evidence is everywhere. If you can't relate to any of this, here is a sure way to find it.

- Do you think you're especially attractive?
- Are you supercompetitive? Do you hate to lose? (And do you usually win?)
- Would you say you are self-confident? *half self confident*

There it is again: a life that is always judged by others. The only difference is that, at least for the moment, the judges score you highly. Yet it is even more complicated. Deep down those who are super self-confident don't believe the judges' high scores. They feel like failures—frauds who are barely fooling other people. Do you think beautiful celebrities struggle with feeling judged and unaccepted by others? Count on it.

Some people seem more self-confident or at least less self-conscious than others. It's hard to know exactly why, but everyone can easily recall times when they withered under the rejection (or possible rejection) of other people.

I know, I know. You were trying to manage this perfectly common experience by ignoring it, and somebody (me) comes along and makes an issue out of it. But my purpose is not to make you miserable. Stick with it, because this particular problem is actually a window into the mysteries of the universe. It takes you directly to three questions that every human being must answer: Who am I? Who is God? and Who are you? And there is no way I would invite you down this road unless the road was very good.

2

It's Everywhere

Skip ahead if you want, but it might be worth your time to take a few more minutes to identify how we can be ruled by the question, What will you think about me?

Here's an interesting one. Did you know that there is a repeating theme in artwork around the world? It is also common in scary movies, hallucinations, and dreams. Eyes. Eyes that follow you. Eyes that see you but can't be seen. There's a reason this image keeps showing up: we are afraid to be seen—we don't want others to see our shortcomings—but we don't mind being the ones who see.

Do you notice how you act differently when someone is watching versus when you think you're alone? You might play a mean air guitar in your bedroom, but most of us wouldn't display this talent in public. "Peer pressure" is the old name for this phenomenon. Peer pressure usually means that the influence of friends is so strong that you wind up doing things you normally wouldn't do to gain acceptance. Using drugs is the classic example, but you could broaden peer pressure to include anything you would do with your friends, but not if a parent, authority figure, or God were present. Some people use normal language with adults and teachers but profanity with friends. Most people wouldn't want their daily lives videotaped and replayed for their parents or pastor.

So keep looking for it. Try to come up with an example from, say, the last hour or so. And don't limit it to actual pressure from other people. Peer pressure doesn't mean that people are threatening to never talk to you again if you refuse to do something. That rarely happens. Peer pressure comes from within *you*. You want to be accepted and liked. It's more about what you want than what other people actually say, do, or think. Does that make sense? Any examples come to you? *You have to look confident! You need to smile! You have to be strong and encouraging! You have to know what to say*

Here is something to keep in mind. If you glance into the future, you'll see that this problem doesn't fade with time. In fact, if you don't do anything with it now, it gets worse. Mothers are always comparing themselves to other mothers and feeling inferior. Men are always jockeying for prestige and significance. People older than forty talk about codependency, which is a 1980s code word for being controlled by the opinions of others. A more recent name is "cosmetic surgery." This is an adult obsession because other people might be watching and judging. It's no longer called peer pressure though. It goes undercover as "low self-esteem," "depression," or "wanting to look healthy," all of which mean, "I will die if you think I am unattractive." People say they are doing it for themselves, and they are right. They are doing it so they can feel confident that *you think* they still look good.

The problem is within you and me, but the world around us makes it worse. For example, American culture is preoccupied with *personal* happiness, *personal* success, and *personal* fulfillment. This means that our goal in life is to feel good about ourselves, and to feel good about ourselves we need some key people to feel good about us. When we actually say that, it sounds horribly superficial, but sometimes there seem to be very few alternative ways of living. Add to this how families are fragmented and friends can move away. There seems to be nothing larger than ourselves to rely on. You will want to both fit in and stand out.

Modern advertising depends on this problem. Do you know what most advertisers get you to ask? *What will others think of you?* Try this product and you will be cooler, more popular, more cutting edge, and more sexually attractive. Or you will at least fit in better than you do now. Advertising appeals to your allegiance to the opinions of others. Advertisers pay good money to send you a message, and they aren't stupid. They know something about you and what you live for. Any particular advertisements come to mind? *Olay, CoverGirl Perfum,*

It's everywhere. Walk through the streets of New Delhi or Johannesburg, and you'll hear kids talking about parents who are too strict. Guys will be talking about girls, making fun of each other, trying to outdo each other with loud bodily noises. Girls will be talking about guys, telling secrets, and having daily dramas. And everyone will be concerned about what people think of them.

Consider one very sad example. In both Western and Eastern cultures you will find far too much suicide among teens and people in their twenties. Along with car accidents, it is the top killer among teens. In Western countries such as the United States, teens consider suicide because they feel like unloved failures in the eyes of others. In Asia teens consider suicide because they have brought shame on their families, or they have lost face before others. What do others think about me?

Do you remember the first day of junior high or middle school? Sometimes life can feel like one first day of school after another. Along with your concerns about which teachers you would get and how you would find the right classroom were two questions: "How can I fit in?" and its close companion, "How can I stand out?" Your self-consciousness kept growing until you finally found a group that you could sit with at lunch. That's the way it is. Once you break into the teen years, your view of yourself rises and falls on the basis of your own popularity or successes. Unchecked, it continues until the day you die.

Peer pressure, codependency, shame, low self-esteem—these are some of the words used to identify how you can be controlled by the perceived opinions of others. You could even use the phrase "fear of other people" to describe the experience. When you fear something you are controlled by it. If you fear people, you are controlled by people. It's as if the opinions of other people are a threat to you. You are always looking for ways to ward off their life-threatening rejection.

But even now we can find hints of a better way. For example, have you ever been in a group that made you feel like you were part of something bigger than just yourself? Perhaps it was a sports team, a school play, your family, your church, a mission trip, or a political action group. In that group you had a cause that seemed more important than individual recognition. As you look back on that experience, do you remember what a pleasant relief it was to think less frequently about you and your personal success and more about others and the larger team goals? Now if we could just find something bigger to believe in.

The Problem
The Heart of the Matter
Who Is God?
Who Am I?
Who Are They?

The Heart of the Matter

When in doubt, look at what's going on inside you. That's always good advice. Chances are that the problem is not so much the eyes of other people as it is something in you. You want something, and you want it badly. With that in mind, you are going to take a short tour of the things that motivate you—the things you live for. But since your own heart can be a difficult place to navigate and see clearly, you need the Bible to show the way. It gives you a fully functioning instrument panel as you consider the question, Who am I?

3

Three Questions

So much of life comes down to the following three questions:

Who is God?
Who am I?
Who are these other people?

You might not wake up in the morning with these questions on your mind. In fact, you might *never* have asked these questions. But, as a human being, those questions are part of your DNA. You will find them sneaking around in your anger, happiness, contentment, jealousy, sadness, fear, guilt, cutting, sense of purpose, life meaning, decision making, moral choices about sex, friendships, school, work, and so on. Notice, for example, how jealousy answers these questions.

Who is God?
  "He is someone who should give me what I want."

Who am I?
  "I deserve better—better looks, better athletic ability, a better boyfriend or girlfriend."

"I am a judge who is authorized to stand over others."

Who are these other people?

"They are below me. They have things that I deserve more than them."

Sadness or depression? Listen and you will hear their answers too.

Who is God?

"He is far away and doesn't care."

"He is someone who didn't give me what I wanted."

"He could never forgive me for what I have done."

Who am I?

"I am nothing, literally nothing. It isn't that I am trash; I am just nothing."

"I am needy, and I haven't gotten what I need."

"I am alone."

"I am God. I deserved something and I didn't get it."

Who are these other people?

"They are my life. I put my hope in them, and they let me down."

"They don't care, so I am trying not to care about them, but it isn't working."

"They can't be trusted."

You can see what's happening. You already have answers to these questions. You just have to uncover them. You might know some right answers, such as "I am a child of God." But our hearts are complicated. The right answer is rarely your only answer. Instead, you usually have at least two sets of answers: those that are "right," and those that actually guide the way you live. To discover your real answers to these questions, watch how you live. In particular, track your emotions. Look for what makes you upset, depressed, angry, and anxious, or what makes you happy, calm, excited, and peaceful.

Once you settle into one of your less comfortable moods, who do you say God *really* is?

- Angry
- Far away and not aware of what you are doing in secret
- Far away and uncaring about what is bothering you
- Picky
- Unfair

What about other people? Who are they?

- Objects you manipulate so that they serve you
- Protectors
- Threats
- Jerks
- Things that can make you feel really good or really bad
- Idols that you worship

And you? Who are you? Try to capture your view of yourself with a picture. If the picture is "child of God" don't stop there. Find some others.

- I am alone, living behind thick walls. I can see out, and everyone else looks normal, but I am isolated.
- I am a leper who has to live with other lepers far away from everyone else.
- I am the black sheep—unwanted, standing out in a bad way and not fitting in.
- I feel like a baby bird, vulnerable, needy, waiting to be pushed out of the nest.
- I am a piece of a puzzle, happy to fit in but not stand out.

Any you would add?

When it comes to being controlled by the opinions of others—the fear of man—there is one image that fits most of us: a vessel, cup, bowl, or some kind of container. Listen for words such as *need*, *want*, and *empty*. They hint that we want to be filled with something that only other people can give us. Ever feel empty?

Sometimes when I see the guilt and stupidness I have in me. Also when I think no one is truly my friend.

Any thoughts on what you think would fill you?

Dependable friends, a strong talent

Picture a cup, something like the animated walking teacups of Walt Disney's *Beauty and the Beast*. There is already something in it; call it self-esteem for now. Some people have more, some less, but no one feels like they have much. You waddle around, hoping that no one bumps you so hard that everything spills out. You also hope that someone close by is in the shape of a pitcher so you can be filled. What would cause a spill?

"Failur"

"Loser!"

"We decided not to hire you."

"We regret to inform you that you weren't accepted to . . ."

"Can't you do anything right?!"

What would fill you up?

"Great (fill in talent here)"

"Nice outfit."

"Awesome game!"

"Good job."

"I love you."

"I love you" fills you up best. Sometimes it is enough to hear it from a parent. More often, parents can't fill you with their words of affection, though they certainly can cause you to spill all over the place with words of rejection. The job of filling you is usually reserved for your peers. Get an "I love you," or even an "I really like you," from the right person, and life is wonderful. You feel great. Full. Who cares if someone bumps into you? "I love you" is high-octane fuel for your self-esteem.

If you *don't* get filled, bad things happen. You wander around with a case of the blues, though you might not even realize it. Some people try to fill themselves with other things: achievements, sex, drugs, music, video games, Internet porn, and fantasy. But none of it really works. Even if you receive love it doesn't work for too long. It is like a drug that fills you for awhile—about an hour or so—and then you need more. And there will be days when you feel so bad that even "I love you" won't make any difference. Either your cup has a leak in it, or you weren't intended to live like a cup. Which one do you think it is? (Both answers are correct, so you don't have to worry about getting the wrong answer.) *My cup has a leak in, t*

Do you have any ideas why life as a love cup doesn't work?
Because we aren't perfect, It is not what God intended love to be

There is nothing wrong with wanting love. It would be positively inhuman not to want it. The problem comes when we desire it too much—when our desire for love becomes the center of life—which, when you think about it, makes us the center of our own lives. The problem is when we want to *be* loved more than we want to love. If only life could be a little bit less about us.

Then it gets worse. When we live as love cups, we will get hurt. There is no doubt about that. We can never get filled enough. When the hurts pile up, we feel ashamed and protect ourselves. We hide behind masks. You can't let others see you or really know you. You try to spruce up your facade with grades, thinness, or some other accomplishment, but you never feel covered up enough. When other people are staring, it's as if they can see through the mask. So you move on to something less revealing—if masks won't work maybe walls will. But walls have problems of their own. Have you ever experienced the transition from love cup (or approval cup or success cup or . . .) to mask to walls? We all have, so what was it like for you?

I have Wtts I was like the things went from ok to worse in 0 - 10 minutes but I just seemed very distant

What masks do you wear the most?
- *Ken Humor*
- Intelligence
- Athletics
- Popularity
- Creativity, being different
- *Confidence*

One problem with masks and walls is that, though their purpose is to protect you from hurt, they hurt you even more because they don't allow relationships. You can't have a deeper relationship if you won't allow yourself to be known. All this leads to a dead end: if you allow people to know you, you get hurt; if you protect yourself from people, you get hurt. It ends in misery. But there is another way. This better way allows us to be open and honest and part of a community where we don't have to put up self-defensive walls. Ever been there? Have you ever had the pleasure of being open with another person?

Many many times. with friends and family

Think about it. What's better than having relationships that let you be yourself? If you have ever experienced that, be sure to thank those people. *Yes I will*

4

Your Family Tree

Of those three questions—about who God is, who others are, and who you are—keep thinking more deeply about who *you* are. In order to do that, you need a guide, and for this journey, the Bible is the only one that is reliable.

Pause for just a second. Do you remember that you have more answers than you realize to questions about God, yourself, and other people? The same thing is true with the Bible. If the Bible is going to be your guide, you might want to consider what you think about that guide—what you really think.

The Bible is God's communication to you. You might already know that, but there is more. For example, if you really believed it was the God of the universe speaking you would probably read it more often. What else is the Bible to you?

- An old history book that is hard to understand and doesn't speak to today's issues?
- A pin prick to your conscience that makes you feel guilty?
- Jesus and some rules?
- A book that drains the fun out of everything?

- Medicine that tastes bad, but somewhere in the way distant future, will be good for you?

• Treasure with a point

Here is the real reality. The Bible is *about* God and *by* God. Stop. That's a big deal. Are you on board? If so, let's take one more step. In the Bible, God speaks to everything in a better and more attractive way than anyone or anything else can, and you are going to love what he says. Any argument with this? Do you live as if this is true?

Yes all the way

Let's keep going. The Bible isn't just about heaven and only for the by-and-by. It is gritty and real. It is about messed-up people and the way God pursues them. The Bible describes real life—with its ups and downs and our stubborn quests for independence—better than anything else. It also shows you how to live the way you were intended to live. What do you think of when you hear the phrase "the way you were intended to live"? What is your first impression? Is it "don't do this, but do that"? Anything else? It says to me that we are all made one certian way un igly.

Actually, "the way you were intended to live" means something much better than "do this, don't do that." Think about an unsaddled horse at full gallop or a dolphin on a cresting wave. Your guess is that those animals find pleasure in doing what they were intended to do. You can see it in dogs too. Put a few kids in a room with a sheep-dog and the dog has the time of its life. It circles the children-sheep and keeps them in a tight circle until one of them finally cries. This doesn't bother the sheepdog at all because he is too happy doing what he was intended to do. If the Bible is really the Word of God, and God is the one who created you, then the Bible can show you how you were intended to live. Read it, get the hang of it, and live it, and you will feel like a fully alive human being. Are you okay with this so far? Any objections? *nope totally ok*

What difference would it make if you believed that the Bible gave explanations and solutions for our brokenness so that we all could be everything God intended? How might this affect you every day? *IT would make us or me feel that I was to dumb to figure it out on my own. It would make us extreamly lazy*

Let's jump in and listen to how God speaks about the opinions of others. Step one? Find the problem. You have already done that with yourself; now let's find some ancient, kindred spirits. Search for people in the Bible who are just like you because they were dominated by what other people could do to them or even just think about them.

Abraham and Isaac

You get some hints of this modern problem in a short story about Abraham. There was a famine in the land, and he and his family went down to Egypt because there was food available there. This, however, created another problem for Abraham. Apparently, Pharaoh, the ruler of Egypt, collected women, and Abraham's wife Sarah was attractive. Afraid that Pharaoh might kill him in order to have Sarah for the royal harem, Abraham told Sarah to say that she was his sister. So she did, and she was taken into Pharaoh's palace. Only God's miraculous deliverance kept her safe (Genesis 12).

No matter how you figure this story, it's not good. Abraham could have trusted God rather than put his wife at such risk. Instead, the potential threat of other people led him to take reckless action.

Who am I? "I am small and empty. I need what only Pharaoh can
give me."
Who are other people? "They are threats to my life. They are huge."
Who is God? "I don't really know. I think he must be far away,
and he has left me on my own."

Not one to learn a lesson, at least with this particular problem,
Abraham did the same thing a few years later with a much less dan-
gerous king whose name was Abimelech (Genesis 20). Then, in a case
of the apple not falling far from the tree, Abraham's son Isaac did the
same thing with a descendant of Abimelech (Genesis 26).

You get the sense that this fear of other people thing is instinctive
to human nature. People have given in to it for a long time, and they
don't tend to learn quickly.

Israel and Her Enemies

The classic story of being controlled by the possible actions of other
people is when God's people, the Israelites, sent out spies into the
land God had promised them. Listen to their pitiful report.

"We can't attack those people; they are stronger than we are. . . .
The land we explored devours those living in it. All the people
we saw there are of great size. We saw the Nephilim there (the
descendants of Anak come from the Nephilim). We seemed
like grasshoppers in our own eyes, and we looked the same to
them." (Numbers 13:31–33)

God had just given his people a mighty victory over Egypt, the stron-
gest nation in the world, without requiring them to pick up a weapon.
Now they are describing themselves as grasshoppers among giants.

Who am I? "A grasshopper! I am a mere insect. I am an orphan
alone in the universe."
Who is God? "Small. Powerless. Only one god among many."

Who are they? "Giants who devour. They are Gods!"

A weak moment? After all, doesn't everyone have their fears? Yes, it is understandable, but in this story it is inexcusable. God himself diagnosed the real problem: the people were holding him in contempt (Numbers 14:11). Their cowardice was actually an expression of hatred toward God that ignored his previously displayed power. They completely disregarded what God said to them and decided to do things without him, as if that were possible. It makes you feel that your own struggle isn't so bad in comparison. But don't get too comfortable yet.

In this story nobody is too worried about standing out or fitting in. They were at a more primitive place. Peer pressure would have been a luxury. They were just freaked out by what other people might do to them, and in their freaked-out state, they were answering the three basic questions of life. We understand that.

It is the idea of contempt that is surprising. God diagnosed the people's problem as contempt toward *him*. That seems a little harsh, especially since the people never really mentioned God at all. If they were upset with anyone, they were upset with their leaders who they believed had gotten them into the mess. But God said that their decision to avoid "giants" was really about him.

This one is important. We can be saying things *about* God and *to* God and not even know it. It's like when your parents told you to do something, and you did something else. You never really thought that you were saying to your parents, "I hate you, and I am going to do what I want." You just wanted to do something with your friends. Your actions, however, were against your parents. The Bible picks up this connection in other places too. For example, you can't say that you love God while you hate someone else (James 4:1–4; 1 John 4:20). If you love God, you love other people.

Here is the rule: the way you live reveals what you really think about God, and there are times when it isn't pretty. Try to find an illustration of that from your own life. You might not be thinking about God all the time, but everything you do is about him. Look at the way you treat people. Look at your secret and private world. Look at your worries. Listen to your life and see what you are saying about God.

>*I am bored.*
>>What does that have to do with God? I am saying that the world is basically random. There is no real purpose for anything. God is not doing anything.

>*I am undone thinking about the future.*
>>I am saying that I am alone, and God doesn't care.

>*I hate her.*
>>As 1 John says, if I hate other people, I am standing in judgment of God, and I am saying, "How dare you not make the world the way I want it!"

The good news is that you can be faithless and go your own way, even unconsciously, but God remains faithful. He pursues you (2 Timothy 2:13). To pursue people who don't like you is not very human, but God is God. Be sure to never confuse what God does with what you think a regular human being would do. If you have ever read the New Testament, you will find yourself laughing at times because you were expecting Jesus to act as you or a fairly good human being would, but he inevitably acts very differently. If Jesus doesn't surprise you, then you haven't met him yet.

Jeremiah's Trees

Back to a few more stories. Have you ever heard people say, "There are two kinds of people in the world"? You are either a cat person or a dog person, introvert or extrovert, for hip-hop or against it. The prophet Jeremiah gives a version of this too. There are two kinds of people: you either trust in people, or you trust in God.

>"Cursed is the one who trusts in man, who depends on flesh for his strength and whose heart turns away from the LORD. He will be like a bush in the wastelands; he will not see prosperity

when it comes. He will dwell in the parched places of the desert, in a salt land where no one lives.

"But blessed is the man who trusts in the LORD, whose confidence is in him. He will be like a tree planted by the water that sends out its roots by the stream. It does not fear when heat comes; its leaves are always green. It has no worries in a year of drought and never fails to bear fruit." (Jeremiah 17:5–8)

Don't forget where we are. We have identified how everyone can be controlled by the opinions—the eyes—of other people. We want both to blend in and to be noticed. We are cups who want something from others. We want approval, acceptance, and love. The problem comes when we want those things too much. It is one thing to want people to like you. It is something else to *live* for the approval or love of someone or some group.

You want to be liked, loved, appreciated, and successful. Who doesn't? You *need* to be liked, loved, appreciated, and successful. Now we have a problem. You will be controlled by the thing that you need.

At first the short stroll from *want* to *need* doesn't seem like a big deal. But if you want something, you . . . you simply want it. You are happy to get it, disappointed if you don't. If you *need* something, you *must* have it in order to live. You are alive if you get it, as good as dead if you don't. There is a big difference between the two. Your wants, which we could also call *desires*, are fine when fenced in, yet they are always itching to get loose. When they do, watch out. Life becomes about you and your desires, and you look to other people to satisfy those desires. To use Jeremiah's language, when your desires run amok, you put your trust in other people, which means that you are not putting your trust in God. Instead, other people rule you; God doesn't. Other people actually become your god. Got all that? There is more going on inside of you than you thought. Think of a time when you put your trust in people instead of God? What was the result?

Now you can understand why you need the Bible as a guide. The Bible doesn't mess around on the surface. It gets to the very heart of your heart. Already this little expedition is going much further than you can go on your own. Anyone can see that we can be controlled by other people. There are dozens of books on it. But it takes God's Word to take us into these deeper mysteries.

You trust in something. You can't help it. You are a creature who can't make it through life on your own. You either trust in God or you trust in people. Of course, you trust in more things than just people. The following is just a short list of things you might trust in:

- Grades
- Intelligence
- Athletic ability
- Attractiveness
- Family
- Friends
- Racial or cultural identity
- Health
- Possessions—a car, musical instrument, computer, etc.

But when you look at those things more closely, they usually get back to what people think of you.

- You want good grades so you can be a success in the eyes of others.
- You trust in your abilities so you can look good in the eyes of others.
- You trust in your possessions because they give you an identity. You think they let you fit in with others or stand out above them.

Why do you think you trust in them? What do they have that you want?

If you listen to popular songs, we trust people because they have something very important to us: love. There's the cup. We feel empty and parched. We waddle up to other people and want them to fill us with love. Does that make sense? If not, give an explanation for why you want the things you want.

Now, on to the New Testament.

Jesus' Warning to His Disciples

When Jesus sent his disciples out for the first time he gave them a rousing pep talk, and he included a warning that sounds a little harsh: "Do not be afraid of those who kill the body but cannot kill the soul. Rather, be afraid of the One who can destroy both soul and body in hell" (Matthew 10:28).

The disciples were commissioned to announce the arrival of a new kingdom and the new King—Jesus himself—and people were not going to like it. Instead of welcoming the messengers, the people would criticize and threaten them. That is why Jesus prepared the disciples for their mission. Essentially he was saying,

> "You are going to preach an unpopular message. Rejection is bound to come. Every hour you will be faced with the question, 'Who will I fear?' Or, to put it another way, 'Who will I trust?' The answer won't be easy for you. These are, after all, your people, and you want to be part of them. But fear God more than people."

You will either fear God or other people. There are no other alternatives.

Have you ever noticed how hard it is to talk to other people about Jesus? One reason this is a challenge is that Jesus never makes you more popular. Talk about Jesus and many people begin to roll their eyes and think that you are a fanatic. Or worse, they will think you are out of step with current trends. They will think that you are foolish because you base your entire life on someone's death and resurrection. Have you ever seen this happen? Are you afraid that it could happen?

It is easier to talk about Jesus on a mission trip in a foreign country than it is to talk about Jesus to your friends. It might even be easier to die for Jesus than to speak about him to others and be rejected. Would you agree? If not, why not?

Peter Denies Knowing Jesus

The best known story about cowing to the opinions of others is when Peter denied even knowing Jesus.

> Now Peter was sitting out in the courtyard, and a servant girl came to him. "You also were with Jesus of Galilee," she said. But he denied it before them all. "I don't know what you're talking about," he said.
>
> Then he went out to the gateway, where another girl saw him and said to the people there, "This fellow was with Jesus of Nazareth." He denied it again, with an oath: "I don't know the man!"
>
> After a little while, those standing there went up to Peter and said, "Surely you are one of them, for your accent gives you away." Then he began to call down curses on himself and he swore to them, "I don't know the man!"

Immediately a rooster crowed. Then Peter remembered the
word Jesus had spoken: "Before the rooster crows, you will dis-
own me three times." And he went outside and wept bitterly.
(Matthew 26:69–75)

Imagine it. Your best friend doesn't just dump you but says that he
or she doesn't even *know* you and is willing to swear to it. Why would
Peter do such a thing? Probably because he was scared of what the Jewish leaders might do to him. He knew that the sentence of death was
in the air, and he wanted to be as far from it as possible. But still, that
doesn't make it any better. Plus, he had three chances to get it right.
Maybe you haven't sworn that you don't know Jesus, but chances are
you aren't a super-bold evangelist who couldn't care less about potential rejection. More likely, you can relate to Peter every day.

In the face of such rejection, you would expect Jesus to be completely ticked off and never speak to Peter again. That would be only
fair. But Jesus doesn't act according to our expectations. How did
Jesus respond to Peter after his betrayal? After Jesus' resurrection,
he made a beeline to Peter and, with a deft touch, lovingly handled
what must have been a horribly awkward situation.

"Simon [Peter] son of John, do you truly love me more than these
[other disciples]?" (John 21:15). A curious question given the circum-
stances. Peter answered that he did indeed love Jesus. Jesus then said,
"Take care of my sheep." Jesus was telling Peter that he was still a
valued disciple with a mission. Peter's denial was not enough to cause
Jesus to cast him away. That is another way of saying that there is
nothing you can do that is enough for Jesus to cast *you* away.

What was odd was that Jesus asked the question again. Peter responded with the same answer. Even more peculiar was that Jesus
asked *almost* the same question a third time. Peter, perplexed, gave
the same answer. Why did Jesus do this? At some point Peter must
have put it together. "Let me see. Why did Jesus ask me three times
if I loved him? And why did he follow those questions with 'feed my
sheep'? He didn't rebuke me about my denials. He didn't even say

anything about them. Oh, yes he did. I denied him three times. He matched my three denials with his three-fold acceptance. Amazing! That is the way I want to treat others."

There are many other stories. These are just some of the noteworthy ones. What do they say about what people really believe?

What does Peter's story say about Jesus?

What do the stories say about you?

Since a lot of information is flooding in, here is a quick summary. You can be easily controlled by the opinions of others. Why? You want them to fill you with something. They have something you feel you need. You think that they might have living water.

When your wants become needs, it means that you have put your trust in people. They have become like a god to you. Yet, for some reason, the true God is patient with you. Although you might reject him, he doesn't reject you. And this is everyone's story.

5

Worshipers

You have a few different words you have been considering—wants, needs, desires, trust, fear, love. You also have a few different images rumbling around in your head—eyes that watch you, cups that leak, grasshoppers among giants, masks that don't fully cover, walls that don't protect. Here is one more image that will make everything even more vivid and a little scary.

Who am I? I am a worshiper. Can you see it? There we are bowing down at the altar of fitting in, standing out, the opinions of others, or whatever else you want to call it. U2 used this image in the lyrics to the song "Mysterious Ways": "If you want to kiss the sky, better learn how to kneel. On your knees, boy!"

We are all kneeling and bowing down before something. The thing or person you trust in is actually the object of your worship. Look carefully and you will see that what started off as a small concern about the opinions of other people has been supersized. It became the center of your life. When your desire for acceptance, love, and approval grows like this, you are actually worshiping other people. They become idols with legs.

"He worships the ground she walks on."

"She is obsessed with him."

It sounds like you are part of a religious cult, doesn't it? And that's not far from the truth.

Since this is so important to understand, let's get the story that lies behind it. You can pick it up during the time the Israelites were leaving Egypt. Just about everything you ever needed to know about human beings can be found in this story. Israel's story is *your* story.

To be very brief, the Israelites were slaves in Egypt, and God surprised them with an amazing deliverance. How did they express their thanks? The people responded by following other gods or idols. It only took a couple of days or so for their idolatrous instincts to kick in. It happened while Moses was atop Mount Sinai, having been summoned by the Lord. The people became a little anxious that their leader was gone longer than anticipated, so they did what most human beings do. They built an idol—in this case, a golden calf—and they began to worship it.

> [Moses] said to Aaron, "What did these people do to you, that you led them into such great sin?"
>
> "Do not be angry, my lord," Aaron answered. "You know how prone these people are to evil. They said to me, 'Make us gods who will go before us. As for this fellow Moses who brought us up out of Egypt, we don't know what has happened to him.' So I told them, 'Whoever has any gold jewelry, take it off.' *Then they gave me the gold, and I threw it into the fire, and out came this calf!*" (Exodus 32:21–24, emphasis added)

This has to be one of the silliest things ever said. "We were minding our own business, a few people threw some things on the fire, and—*voila!*—out popped an idol. It's all very odd, Moses."

Go almost anywhere in the world and you will find idols. If you come from a country that doesn't have idols in every house, idolatry might seem strange. But people are people. You are more like the Punjabi who worship Rama than you think. Everyone is bowing down to something. In the United States, we keep one of our idols— aka "money"—safe in banks and invested in stocks. The other idols are walking around among us. They are other people.

You were walking along, minding your own business. You threw a few things on the fire to keep warm when suddenly out popped a gold statue in the shape of a person, or a group of people, and it became the center of your life. Before you knew it you were on your knees. That is the story in Ancient Israel. It is the story in your school. It is the story in your work. It is your story. Atheist or Christian, it is your story.

If you have put your trust in Jesus, you might protest a bit and say that Jesus is the object of your worship. But life is more complicated than it first appears. Even if you worship Jesus Christ and say that he alone is King, you can easily drift into mixed allegiances. For example, the Israelites only trusted God for *some* things. He was God over the Nile River, frogs, and locusts because he demonstrated that before the Israelites left Egypt. He was God of the mountains, because that was where he was meeting with Moses. But was he God of the valleys? Was he the God of fertility who would increase the people's cattle and flocks? They weren't so sure. So, to cover all their bases, they split their allegiances. It's like putting some money in one stock and the rest in another, just in case one goes bad. Can you see those divided allegiances in yourself? Worry is one example. Plain old disobedience is another.

Sometimes we trust him, sometimes we don't. What do you trust God for? What *don't* you trust God for?

That leads us to the next question: How do I get out of this mess? How do I change? There will be answers later, but maybe you already have ideas on how it happens. Do you ever think about change as a real possibility?

How have you changed for the better?

Any ideas on how you can actually change yourself? How do you do it?

6

More on Worship

Since the notion of worship is different from the way we normally think, let's stay with it a little longer. Picture it. An idol (what others think about you) that sometimes you put it in the closet but is usually right at the center of your life. What does your worship look like? Anxiety, despair, shopping, primping, acting like someone you aren't, acting stupid when you are smart, or acting like you don't care when you do? Why do you do it? You are hoping that, if you worship it correctly, the idol will give you what you want. But idols are notoriously slow in responding.

There are two types of worship: false worship and true worship. When you think of false worship, you think about people physically bowing down to a statue. Yet, as you have learned, that is only a fraction of the false worship that goes on. Most of it goes on in your heart, in the privacy of your own thoughts. For example, jealousy means you want something badly, and wanting something badly is the same thing as worshiping it. Some people might say that you are addicted to it, which means that you are on your knees, face down, worshiping the thing you want. Track down your anger and you will discover what you worship. You want something badly! You need it! You get mad when you don't get it! You worship it.

True worship, of course, has to do with God. When you think of good or true worship you probably think about praise songs and hymns. In a church service, the "worship" time is usually when everyone sings, though some churches might say, "Let's continue our worship with our tithes and offerings." But worship extends far beyond the walls of a church. When you trust in Jesus rather than your reputation, and you follow him in love and obedience, even when it hurts, then you are truly worshiping.

Here is a way to talk about both false and true worship: we worship what we love.

- Love music above all else; it will be your obsession and will hurt your relationships.
- Love a particular person above all else; he or she will be your obsession. Your moods will rise and fall depending on how that person treats you or how much time you spend together.
- Love the approval, acceptance, or love of other people; they will be like a god to you and control your life.

To paraphrase Jeremiah 17, all your choices fall into one of two categories: either you do something because you worship God and love him above all else, or you worship other people and love what they might give you. What would you say you love most? Follow the track of your emotions—your happiness, sadness, hopelessness, despair, and anger—then you will find what you love.

Why do you think it's so easy to love other things more than Jesus? Isn't it especially strange since he created all good things, including the things you worship?

Do you ever think about what it means to love Jesus?

There is something sneaky about false worship. Usually it starts innocently and progresses gradually. Think about ancient Israel again. They were warned not to associate with the neighboring idolaters. But at some point they were talking over the backyard fence and noticed that idolaters weren't bogeymen, so they began to hang out with them. Such socializing didn't seem like it was a big deal. Little did they realize that they were dipping their toes in the water of idolatry. They were testing it before they jumped in. It's not that they *consciously* were forsaking the true God. It was that they wanted to insure themselves against hard times. Their neighbors' gods promised good crops and prosperity. Couldn't hurt to try them, could it?

But it does hurt. It's like being married and then adding a second wife or husband just in case the first one doesn't quite satisfy all your needs. You can say that you love your first spouse, and you might even believe that, but your first spouse won't. Your first spouse knows your actions are an outright rejection and betrayal. You renounce your first spouse by taking another.

That's what happens in your relationship with God. That's why the Bible says that pursuing your own desires is the same as betraying God. The following passage diagnoses the real cause of your conflicts with your friends and your parents, and then takes you right to its roots in your rejection of God:

What causes fights and quarrels among you? Don't they come from your desires that battle within you? You want something but don't get it. You kill and covet, but you cannot have what you want. You quarrel and fight. You do not have, because you do not ask God. When you ask, you do not receive, because you ask with wrong motives, that you may spend what you get on your pleasures.

You adulterous people, *don't you know that friendship with the world is hatred toward God? Anyone who chooses to be a friend of the world becomes an enemy of God.* (James 4:1–5, emphasis added)

Ouch. Strong words! When you are angry with someone, you certainly aren't consciously thinking about God. You are just thinking that the other person is wrong. It is all very simple. But our hearts are busier than that. Underneath our quarrels are our desires—the things that we love. And whenever we love our desires, we hate God. It sounds horrible to even think, but it is true. Whenever we are owned by our desires, we are friends with the world—which is shorthand in the Bible for the dark kingdom that is against God's kingdom.

Does that make sense to you? Can you see the connection between everyday behaviors and your relationship with God? Take some time on this one. It will serve you well for the rest of your life to develop a thought process with this hardwired into it. Instead of God being relevant to you only at certain times (such as funerals, really big hurts, and really nasty guilt), you will find that everything in your life ultimately points in his direction. You either love him or hate him.

All this sounds a bit severe, but this is why the Bible makes such a big deal about forgiveness of sins. If you only sin once in a while—when you do something really bad—you are glad that God forgives you. But the rest of the time you don't think about God very much. You don't think you are doing anything too bad, so you don't think you really need God's forgiveness. But if your allegiances are more mixed than you realize—split between worship of God and worship of your desires—then forgiveness of sins is important all the time. When God is relevant all the time, it becomes more natural to be thankful to him.

So, who are you? You are a worshiper. You bow down. That is
   your deepest identity.

What do you worship? Whatever you love the most: God or
   anything other than God.

Why do you worship things other than God? Because you hope
   your idols will give you what you want. You are worshiping
   idols, but you are really worshiping yourself and your desires.
   There is a deep self-centeredness in idolatry: It's all about me.
   I want what I want. I want more. I want to manage my world,
   or at least parts of it, without God.

What is the result of false worship? We become a slave to whatever
   we love. That's what it's like to be controlled by the opinions of
   others: slavery.

Yes, there are dark places in your heart. But you shouldn't be feeling miserable. You should actually feel hopeful. The Bible understands
you—God understands you. He gives you an accurate, true, and honest read on your own heart, and he still doesn't reject you.

In the story of the golden calf, God continued to love his people.
He warned them about idolatry and told them that life would be hard
if they chose that path, but he was not going to leave them. In fact, at
that very time, he revealed more about himself to the people:

The Lord, the Lord, the compassionate and gracious God,
slow to anger, abounding in love and faithfulness, maintaining
love to thousands, and forgiving wickedness, rebellion and sin.
(Exodus 34:6–7)

Moses, who was the first to hear this, did what came naturally. He
worshiped the Lord. There is no reason to run away when your divided worship is exposed. Instead, run toward the One who delights
in forgiving you.

There is one thing you must know about God: he is not like an
ordinary person. If you committed yourself to a person and then gave

your heart to another, the person to whom you first committed your-self would be rightly angry. That person would probably stop the rela-tionship, and for good reason. God, however, is not what you imagine. He is different. He responds in ways that you do not expect.

- You rebel; he pursues.
- You act like he doesn't exist; he forgives you.
- You think that he is not good; he patiently shows his goodness to you until you see that he is good and loves you.

The only way you can change the focus of your worship is to find something even better to focus on. That is your task. For the rest of your life your goal is to be surprised by God to the point that you re-spond like Moses: you worship.

Have you ever had that experience? If so, what was it about God that inspired you? If not, would you like to know God well enough to be able to worship him?

Can you think of anything in the Bible that reminds you that God is far from ordinary? Are there any stories that leave you in awe? If you can't think of any, ask your friends who know the Bible if they have any. Ask a parent. Ask a youth leader or pastor.

It's time to write out a summary. What are you seeing? Are you getting enough light to see the way out? We are talking about being controlled by the opinions of other people—how they can be our god—and we are talking about a way out that is better than you think.

Here is a good way to make certain that you are on the right path. Check to see if the path looks good—really good. When you learn about yourself in a way that helps you to understand who God really is, you will love it. Sure, your heart pops out people-idols. In fact, it mass-produces them. That's not exactly pretty, but when God is working in your life you begin to see things you couldn't otherwise see. You can only see your idols when God turns the lights on for you. That means he is on the move, caring for you, and loving you. So if this is making sense, keep your eyes open. God will be doing even more.

7

When Does a Good Thing Turn Bad?

Is all this going a little too deep? After all, people are not always objects of your worship. Sometimes they are just people. Sometimes you are hanging around with your friends, relaxing, and enjoying one another. That doesn't automatically mean they are a bunch of idols. How can you tell when people have become too big in your life and when they haven't?

False worship usually starts out with good things—people, money, health, work, and comfort. The problem is that we start to love them more than God. Do you enjoy being part of a group? Excellent. You should enjoy it. That is how you were intended to be. You weren't created to be a loner. The problem begins when that group becomes the center of your world, and you start selfishly excluding other people. Or, you get together or go online with them even when you know you should be doing something else. Do you want to be loved? If you didn't, you wouldn't be a human being. But sometimes that desire turns into a five-hundred-pound gorilla that always demands to be fed.

Do you want to be seen as a success? That is a trickier one. Your desire to work hard is certainly a good thing, as is your desire to do things well. But a desire for success can get selfish and idolatrous quickly. When you think about it, the quest for success can sound pretty self-centered. How about wanting a good reputation? Everyone would like that, but the question is why do you want a good reputation? Is it to stand out? A good thing run amok—that is the nature of idolatry.

Since idolatry can masquerade as something innocent, here are some questions that can help you unveil it.

- What do you think you need from other people? That word *need* is usually a camouflaged version of love. What do you love from other people?
- Do you ever find yourself thinking, *I deserve...* or *these are my rights*? What makes you angry or jealous?
- Do you ever think about suicide? What provokes those thoughts? What makes you depressed? Chances are that something other than God is controlling you.
- Fill in the blank: "If only _____, then I would be happy."
- Do you obsess over your failures?
- Do your emotions soar and crash according to what other people might think or say?
- Are you painfully shy?

When does a normal desire cross the line? You can't usually see it happening. It is like when the day turns from dusk to night. Your eyes gradually adjust to the dark and you can't pinpoint the moment it happened. But, once again, it is more complicated than that. Usually, we can't see what's happening because we *close* our eyes. We don't want to see what's really happening. We would prefer to quietly slip away from God's kingdom and walk on the dark side.

So is there any hope? Are you doomed always to slip across that line that separates normal desires from idolatrous ones? It's guaranteed, you can change. God gives you a map that leads away from false worship and on to true worship.

8

A Map

It's time to lay out the path. As you expect, the journey is going to be lifelong. No one really erases our tendency to put our trust in other people. But you'll find that you make progress, and the path is so beautiful you will love the trip even if you stumble occasionally and get a few bruises along the way.

Don't be intimidated by the process. You don't have to be a talented heart inspector. The truth is, the more you plunge into your own heart, the murkier everything looks. But remember, you are doing this with the God who loves you. He doesn't love you because you accurately see the false worship in your heart. He loves you simply because he is love and he loves you. If he loved you because you were idol free, his love would change from day to day. But since he loves you because he is love, his love is constant. As one expression of that love, his Spirit will show you where your desires have led you astray, and the Spirit will lead you back to Jesus Christ.

Turn Around

The first thing you have to do is turn around. If you are living for the praise of other people, the path you are on is dark and hopeless, and ironically you feel alone. Your emotions go off the charts. Sometimes you are way up, other times way down. It all depends on whether your idol is giving you what you want or not. You have to start by turning around.

Where do you turn? Do a 180 and turn back to God. Some people call that repentance. The curious thing about turning back to God is that, once you turn, you don't have to walk for miles to get to the border of God's kingdom. Instead, the boundary line is always just one step away. It doesn't matter how far you have walked in the wrong direction. Once you turn around, God and his kingdom are right in front of you. Go figure; it is another mystery.

There is only one way this could happen though. God must always be pursuing you. No mere mortal would ever do such a thing. If you turn your back on friends or lovers, you might get another chance, but you would have a long walk back from the doghouse. Make a habit of it and they are gone. They will turn their backs on you. God, however, keeps following you in love. He orchestrates events in your life so that you will listen to him. He is always inviting you back. He is always near.

Do you ever worry that you have backslidden so far from God that it will take you the rest of your life just to get back to him—which means that it can't be done? Not true. Just turn to God. Pay more attention to God than to how bad you might feel.

Listen to God

Once you are redirected toward God's kingdom, sit and listen. You thought God's kingdom was all about him telling you what to do, as if God were a cosmic drill sergeant or a grouchy parent. But if you look at some of the great prayers in Scripture, they are prayers that you would know God better.

The apostle Paul says, "I keep asking that the God of our Lord Jesus Christ, the glorious Father, may give you the Spirit of wisdom and revelation, so that you may know him better" (Ephesians 1:17). Do you see what's going on in that verse? Paul is praying that God will help you to know God better. It's like this: imagine you're out with someone amazing—someone you really want to get to know—but you don't quite know what to say. Thankfully your friend comes to your rescue and says, "You could ask me how I like school." The Father helps you know him better.

This is a relationship. In a relationship, people enjoy the opportunity to know each other. God knows you. You, however, don't know God very well, and he is eager to share his innermost thoughts with you.

What does this have to do with the opinions of others? This problem is about your heart loyalties and who wins the battle for your worship. If you are going to change your loyalties or allegiances, the only way you will do it is if you believe God is more attractive than anything in all creation. After all, he is the creator of all things beautiful. If you don't know God, you can't just muster up enthusiasm to turn toward God and hope to keep pointing in that direction. Instead, when you turn toward him, listen carefully for stories *about* God and *by* him that are surprising and beautiful. Everything God says should sound like a wonderfully loving and subversive attack on your old way of living.

Oh, and the question about how to change? This is key: If you have changed in your life, for the better or the worse, there was always a person involved. Can you think of one or two ways you have changed in your life? Can you identify the person who was involved?

God's way of changing you is usually through another person. And if an average mortal can help you change, imagine how much more knowing God can change you. Have you ever had an amazing insight into God's love that left you feeling different, even changed?

If you experienced one of those spiritual moments, did that change continue, or did it burn out? Did you actually accomplish the goals you set for yourself? If it burned out, why do you think it did?

Do you have any ideas on how to avoid that burnout in the future?

Love Other People

As you get to know God, something will happen. You will love him more, and you will want to act like him. Even in a human relationship, if you really respect and love someone, you will naturally take on many of his or her characteristics. Of course, you will still look like you, but discerning people will notice the similarities. Since God is love, the most obvious way you will imitate him will be by loving other people. Up until now, the problem has been that you wanted something *from* other people more than you wanted something *for* other people. You loved yourself more than you loved them. In other words, you were hanging out in your own kingdom and avoiding God's. The path you are taking now will guide you to God's kingdom, a place where you are able to *love* people more than *need love* from them.

How does that sound? If it doesn't sound like a good goal, then consider why. If the kingdom of God doesn't sound absolutely beautiful to you, you will always be finding other things to worship. Don't forget that the Bible teaches you how to be a fully functioning human being, not a broken one. You are going to like it—like dolphins on waves, being what you were intended to be.

Learn Who You Are

There are those three questions that always need your attention.

Who is God?
Who are other people?
Who am I?

Your map will contain some important answers.

Who is God? He is better than you think.
Who are other people? They are people who you can enjoy, serve,
   and love.
But who are you?

So far, you have been a cup, someone who wears masks, a false
worshiper, and a person who wants to grow and change. Yet there is
more. For example, how do you like the idea of being royalty?

To know yourself you must first know *the* royal person, Jesus the
King. He comes close to you, teaches you about himself, invites you to
follow him, and teaches you how to be like him. He knows that he has
set the bar high, but he also knows that you were intended to be like
him, and you won't be happy until you are moving in that direction.
Yes, it might seem impossible at times, but he has given you his Spirit,
who is immensely powerful to equip you for the task ahead.

Who are you? You are somebody who is intended to look like
   Jesus and live for him rather than yourself.

The map is very simple: know God and love others. Yet while this is
simple and accessible to young children, thousands of Christ-follow-
ers keep seeing more depth and breadth in who God is. You too are
part of this group. We are delving into the mysteries of the universe.
In the past, our tendency to be controlled by the opinions or actions
of others has been a riddle without a solution. Now, God has revealed

to us a way out. No one can figure out this riddle on their own. God had to tell us; and since it is God telling us, it gets more profound the more we study it.

Sound good? The journey should be filled with hope, and it ends with joy. If hope and joy are absent, you are on the wrong path. Just turn around and get your bearings. Aim for Jesus Christ. He is the goal. You want to look at your own heart, but you want to get really good at looking toward Jesus.

The Problem
The Heart of the Matter
Who Is God?
Who Am I?
Who Are They?

Who Is God?

When you want to find out how you've gotten into a problem, it's best to start by looking at yourself. When you want to find a way out, it's always best to start with God. Your goal is to know him in such a way that other people will be less awesome in comparison. God is no ordinary person. When people in the Bible were given glimpses of him—face-to-face—they were overwhelmed. You too have an opportunity to know him this way because he has revealed himself in the person of Jesus Christ. Know Jesus and you know God. Feel free to be overwhelmed, in a good way.

9

God Is Holy

"Do not be afraid of those who kill the body but cannot kill the soul. Rather, be afraid of the One who can destroy both soul and body in hell" (Matthew 10:28). Not very pleasant options, at least at first glance: Fear people or fear the Lord. Be afraid of people or be terrorized by the Lord. But "the fear of the Lord" must mean more than mere terror; wise people in the Bible have typically loved to have it.

> Fear the LORD, you his saints, for those who fear him lack nothing. The lions may grow weak and hungry, but those who seek the LORD lack no good thing. Come, my children, listen to me; I will teach you the fear of the LORD. (Psalm 34:9–11)

> The fear of the LORD is the beginning of knowledge, but fools despise wisdom and discipline. (Proverbs 1:7)

> He who fears the LORD has a secure fortress, and for his children it will be a refuge. The fear of the LORD is a fountain of life, turning a man from the snares of death. (Proverbs 14:26–27)

The fear of the LORD leads to life: Then one rests content, untouched by trouble. (Proverbs 19:23)

Now it sounds a little more tempting. "Fear" in Scripture must be a richer experience than we think. Those who fear the Lord are satisfied, content, and safe. Who wouldn't want such things?

There are many ways we respond to God: we love him, serve him, honor him, and bless him. To fear him is one of the most frequent ways we are called to respond to him. If you think about it, fear makes sense. When you fear something it controls you. To fear God means to be controlled by him. So fear is good.

But the reason we are identifying the fear of the Lord is that it points us to God's holiness. God's holiness is the objective. When we want to grow in the fear of the Lord, it begins with God teaching us that he is holy. Notice how "fear" and "regard as holy" are basically the same idea.

The LORD Almighty is the one you are to regard as *holy,* he is the one you are to *fear,* he is the one you are to dread, and he will be a sanctuary. (Isaiah 8:13–14, emphasis added)

What comes to mind when you think of the word *holy?*

Holy means that God is not like you or anyone you know. He is greater than anything or anyone you can imagine. A person might be beautiful, but God is holy in his beauty. You might have a father who isn't always nice, but God is the holy Father—you can count on him. Or you might have a parent who you think is really great, but God is the holy parent. Not even the best of parents match up to him.

Your ways, O God, are holy. What god is so great as our God? (Psalm 77:13)

"To whom will you compare me? Or who is my equal?" says the Holy One. (Isaiah 40:25)

If you go to other countries and see actual idols, you will notice that the idols and gods look a little like superheroes. An extra eye to see better, an elephant tusk for added strength, or winged shoes to make them faster. That's what happens when you make up gods; they look like people, except turbocharged. They aren't holy.

One of the ways you can tell that no one made up the God of the Bible is that no human being could have invented him. He is simply not like any person you could possibly imagine. For example, you probably believe that God forgives you when you do your 180 and turn back to him. Good people might forgive like that. But you might also believe that, if God is going to accept you, you had better be really sorry for what you have done, and you had better swear that you won't do it again. Otherwise, he will get really ticked off.

Do you see what just happened? You thought that God was just like other nice people who forgive you when you are sorry and promise never to do anything bad again. But God is holy. He wants you to know that he is in a league of his own. If he wasn't, there would be no reason to worship him.

Imagine this. You said "I hate you" to someone, and you meant it. Meanwhile, that person invites you into a relationship and rejoices when you come back to him or her (Luke 15:4–7). You can't imagine it, can you? You can imagine being in the doghouse for a long time, and you can imagine a perpetually chilly relationship, but you can't imagine someone loving you *while* you showed hatred. You can't imagine someone being excited to forgive you. If you can't imagine those things, excellent! You are beginning to know God.

Do *you* think God acts just like a human being? (Assume that your answer is yes.) In what ways do you act as though God's love is no better than a mere mortal's? How about his power? His goodness? His patience?

- When I do wrong things in private that I would never do in public, I actually believe that God can't see me when I hide.
- When I feel like I have to be nearly perfect before I can come to him, I believe that he won't forgive and accept me until I have changed myself.
- When I worry about the future, I believe that he is far away and involved in more important matters than my own life.
- _____
  _____
- _____
  _____
- _____
  _____

When the Israelites were forging that golden calf, no doubt they thought that God was limited and finite—just like a person. They didn't think he could be at two places at the same time, because what man was able to do such things? If he was on the mountain with Moses, how could he also be in the valley? He couldn't. Therefore, they reasoned, they should be afraid. Little did they realize that the God who was on the mountain was Lord over the cosmos.

When you know someone who is truly extraordinary, you can't just sit there and do nothing. You have to act! You have to respond. If you go to a great concert, you stomp and clap for an encore. You can't wait to tell your friends. You go online and download some of the artist's music. You read more about the group. And you keep telling people. What do you think might be fitting responses to God?

If one of your responses is that you want to know more about him, that is a fine response.

We are still talking about the fear of other people's opinions. The most powerful treatment for it is to learn the fear of the Lord: to be controlled by God rather than by people. When you have hung out in the throne room of the holy King, you aren't as easily dominated by mere humans who are just like you. If you want the fear of the Lord, you are going to have to know that God is holy. Your goal is to learn about Jesus—the fullest revelation of God to you—be amazed, and want to worship him. When you learn something about God that is really great, tell him. When you try to learn something about him but have a hard time understanding, ask him for more understanding of who he is. In order to put your words on this, try writing down your prayer to the Lord.

10

A Story about the Creator

It is a basic principle: the more you are controlled by God, the less you are controlled by other people. The more you love God, the less you will love the acceptance or recognition of others. So grit your teeth and get to work! Just kidding.

The only way you can love him more is to know him. If you really knew him, you would love him. Sometimes we even say that about other people. "Oh, you will love him. I promise." If you can say that about another person, you can surely say it about the Lord. So sit back and listen. What we are after are stories about God, but we have an agenda. In every story we want to know that he is better or greater than we imagined. He is not a smart, fast, nice human being. He is holy. So think of these stories as holy stories.

The natural place to start is the story that reveals God as Creator. "In the beginning God created . . ." Everyone knows those words from Genesis 1. The problem is that they are a little *too* familiar. You might not get too excited about seeing a brother or sister because they are familiar. You see him or her every day. But when an important (or attractive) visitor stops by, the newness of the visit is exciting. You are definitely paying attention.

Let's try a similar approach to Genesis 1. Let's take a fresh look at it, as if we were hearing it for the first time. The first people to hear this story of creation were Hebrew slaves who were on their way out of Egypt. God gave this account to Moses and he, in turn, gave it to the people. In order to get in the right mood you have to think like a recently liberated Hebrew slave.

> In the beginning God created the heavens and the earth. Now the earth was formless and empty, darkness was over the surface of the deep, and the Spirit of God was hovering over the waters. (Genesis 1:1–2)

Moses has just started to read this and already your mind is reeling. You know about lots of gods from your time in Egypt, but you aren't familiar with one God who created all things. So this is very exciting! The God who just liberated you from the mightiest nation on earth—and without you even picking up a stone or spear—is not a mere local god. He is *the* God. He is over everything and everyone, including the famous sun god of the Egyptians. "This is what the LORD says—your Redeemer, who formed you in the womb: I am the LORD, who has made all things, who alone stretched out the heavens, who spread out the earth *by myself*" (Isaiah 44:24). The Egyptians aren't looking so big all of a sudden.

And regarding that comment about the Spirit hovering, the Spirit was the same one who was hovering over the liberated people as a cloud by day and fire by night (Exodus 13:21). If the Spirit of God was part of the creation of the world, then there wasn't anything to fear if the Spirit was with the people. What can an Egyptian enemy do in the face of their creator?

> And God said, "Let there be light," and there was light. God saw that the light was good, and he separated the light from the darkness. God called the light "day," and the darkness he

called "night." And there was evening, and there was morning—the first day. (Genesis 1:3–5)

There it is. Our God is over the most powerful god of Egypt. No need to worship the sun, no matter how important it is. We worship its creator instead.

It's not surprising that the first thing God causes to appear is light. You are watching the divine painter expressing himself on an earthly canvas, and this painting says something about the painter. Throughout Scripture, God is called light (e.g., Psalm 4:6; 90:8; John 1:4–9). And he makes all this happen with a word. Just a word. It sounds holy, doesn't it!

> And God said, "Let there be an expanse between the waters to separate water from water." So God made the expanse and separated the water under the expanse from the water above it. And it was so. God called the expanse "sky." And there was evening, and there was morning—the second day.
>
> And God said, "Let the water under the sky be gathered to one place, and let dry ground appear." And it was so. God called the dry ground "land," and the gathered waters he called "seas." And God saw that it was good. (Genesis 1:6–10)

Here God is making distinctions within his creation: water, earth, and sky. Everything in creation has its place. It lives within certain boundaries, and we can be glad about that. Otherwise, we would always be dodging asteroids and trying to escape the latest tsunami. God puts constraints on his creation. "Here and no further." You too follow a similar pattern. God gives you boundaries so you know how best to live as a created human being. Sin, by the way, is when you choose to live outside those boundaries.

> Then God said, "Let the land produce vegetation: seed-bearing plants and trees on the land that bear fruit with seed in

it, according to their various kinds." And it was so. The land produced vegetation: plants bearing seed according to their kinds and trees bearing fruit with seed in it according to their kinds. And God saw that it was good. And there was evening, and there was morning—the third day. (Genesis 1:11–13)

It's as if God laid out the dinner plate, filled it, and filled it with a lot.

God makes it very clear that he *created* all the heavenly lights—none of them are gods—and he doesn't even mention the sun by name. After you chuckle at the snub of the famous sun god, you get the feeling that God is very generous. He doesn't dole out little portions; he does things on a large scale. Abundance comes to mind. And that is a good thing because as you look around you in the desert you see nothing. You are looking forward to some of that abundance.

God is not stingy. If you think he is, you don't know the Holy God. If you think that you have to always go outside the boundaries he gives you to find satisfaction, you've overlooked how he fills the earth with good things. If he does it with the earth, you can be sure that he will do it with his people. Sit back and listen to the sheer amount of stuff he pours out into his creation.

And God said, "Let there be lights in the expanse of the sky to separate the day from the night, and let them serve as signs to mark seasons and days and years, and let them be lights in the expanse of the sky to give light on the earth." And it was so. God made two great lights—the greater light to govern the day and the lesser light to govern the night. He also made the stars. God set them in the expanse of the sky to give light on the earth, to govern the day and the night, and to separate light from darkness. And God saw that it was good. And there was evening, and there was morning—the fourth day.

And God said, "Let the water teem with living creatures, and let birds fly above the earth across the expanse of the sky." So God created the great creatures of the sea and every living and moving thing with which the water teems, according to their kinds, and every winged bird according to its kind. And God saw that it was good. God blessed them and said, "Be fruitful and increase in number and fill the water in the seas, and let the birds increase on the earth." And there was evening, and there was morning—the fifth day.

And God said, "Let the land produce living creatures according to their kinds: livestock, creatures that move along the ground, and wild animals, each according to its kind." And it was so. God made the wild animals according to their kinds, the livestock according to their kinds, and all the creatures that move along the ground according to their kinds. And God saw that it was good. (Genesis 1:14–25)

When Europeans first came to American shores they found an abundance of life. Fish were jumping out of the water; whales and dolphins could be seen wherever they looked. Forests were teeming with bear, deer, and all kinds of life. It must have been an awesome sight because they were getting a tiny glimpse of the original creation. Later in the Bible God talks about how life with him is like a sumptuous banquet with a never-ending supply of the very best food (Isaiah 55:1–3). Abundance, satisfaction, and filling the emptiness—that is God's style.

Then God said, "Let us make man in our image, in our likeness, and let them rule over the fish of the sea and the birds of the air, over the livestock, over all the earth, and over all the creatures that move along the ground." So God created man in his own image, in the image of God he created him; male and female he created them. God blessed them and said to them, "Be fruitful and increase in number; fill the earth and subdue it. Rule over the fish of the sea and the birds of the air and over every living creature that moves on the ground."

Then God said, "I give you every seed-bearing plant on the face of the whole earth and every tree that has fruit with seed in it. They will be yours for food. And to all the beasts of the earth and all the birds of the air and all the creatures that move on the ground—everything that has the breath of life in it—I give every green plant for food." And it was so. (Genesis 1:26–30)

He saves the best for last. The crescendo of creation. And all you can do is be amazed. As a slave you know all about the image of God— that's what Pharaoh called himself. He said he was the offspring of the gods, and of course he was the *only* offspring or image of the gods. He was the supreme ruler over all things and all people. He ruled as the gods' representative. But Moses just said that you were God's child, the offspring of royalty. You, a lifelong slave, are created in the image of God.

In one sentence Pharaoh is no longer so high and mighty; he is just like you. And you have gone from being a slave to having a Father who owns the cosmos, which means that you *inherit* the cosmos. The story is only beginning. Within a chapter or two humans start running from the Father and the Father begins to reveal his plan for reclaiming his children. But it is a good start—you are a relatively important person, just as you thought. Other people are more important than you thought, so you treat them with respect. Given this story, the way you were created was to be like your Father, which at least means that you take special interest in those who are marginalized and discarded. Since he takes a special interest in slaves, there is no doubt that he has a unique affection for those who don't fit in.

By the way, you are not just pretending to be a Hebrew slave. This really is your story. God created you. In other words, you belong to him—not to Pharaoh or anyone else. That's the way it is with created things. When you make something it belongs to you. Create a piece of art or even a song and it is yours. If anyone tries to steal it you will get mad and take it back. So you are God's possession. He doesn't want you to belong to anyone else.

There are lots of implications to this one. Any thoughts?

You belong to God and he gives you a mission: be like your Father and represent him in his creation. You are created to make your Father's name known on the earth, which is another way to say that you live for his glory. "Bring my sons from afar and my daughters from the ends of the earth—everyone who is called by my name, whom I created for my glory, whom I formed and made" (Isaiah 43:6–7). What does it mean for you to live for his glory and renown?

Here is another passage that speaks about God as the Creator. God is speaking to renegades who keep going back to idols. God's response it to reveal that he is much bigger than idols, and there is nothing bigger than being the Creator.

"To whom will you compare me? Or who is my equal?" says the Holy One. Lift your eyes and look to the heavens: Who created all these? He who brings out the starry host one by one, and calls them each by name. Because of his great power and mighty strength, not one of them is missing. Why do you say, O Jacob, and complain, O Israel, "My way is hidden from the LORD; my cause is disregarded by my God"? Do you not know? Have you not heard? The LORD is the everlasting God, the Creator of the ends of the earth. He will not grow tired or weary, and his understanding no one can fathom. He gives strength to the weary and increases the power of the weak. Even youths grow tired and weary, and young men stumble and fall; but those who hope in the LORD will renew their strength. They will soar on wings like eagles; they will run and not grow weary, they will walk and not be faint. (Isaiah 40:25–31)

Throughout the Bible, when people are confused and question God's power and goodness—when they have doubts that he is holy—God typically reminds them that he is the Creator who is over all things. His ways are bigger and more sophisticated than we can understand. Try to get a handful of applications from what God says. You could also write down the questions you have.

- When I see beauty in the world, I want to both appreciate it and remember that it is just one small reflection of the God who is holy in his beauty.
- When I see my temptations to worship a person, I must ask myself why I would ever worship a person instead of the Creator of that person?
-

-

-

-

God created you and all things. Do you believe that? Do you *really* believe that? If you do, tell him.

11

Stories from the Re-Creator

When you have been brought into the throne room to spend time with the King and have become known to him by name, the negative opinions of others don't carry as much weight. It's not that you are indifferent toward others and what they think. It is that their opinions can't emotionally derail you, turn you hopelessly inward, and keep you from caring about other people. When you hear that someone you really like also really likes you, the nasty things that a few people think are not going to ruin your day. With that in mind, consider a few more holy stories.

It is one thing to hear *about* a distant king. It is something very different when the King actually comes to your door.

> In the past God spoke to our forefathers through the prophets at many times and in various ways, but in these last days he has spoken to us by his Son, whom he appointed heir of all things, and through whom he made the universe. (Hebrews 1:1–2)

God has determined not just to tell you about himself. He has also entered into human history so he could be "that which was from the beginning, which we have heard, which we have seen with our eyes, which we have looked at and our hands have touched—this we proclaim concerning the Word of life" (1 John 1:1). God definitely wants you to know him.

Jesus, God in the flesh, entered human history. You can watch him go about his everyday life and learn everything you ever wanted to know about God. And here is what is most obvious: he entered history as a servant—your servant. The God of the universe comes to serve those who have turned away from him. Here again, no one could have invented such a god. This is indeed a holy story. If you devise a myth about a great king, the king is always above his people. To enter the king's presence unannounced usually meant death. But the true God came as your servant. That is enough to leave you amazed. It also hints that if he came to serve you, and you follow him, you will be called upon to serve other people. More on that later.

When any king comes as a servant, he might not be immediately recognizable. Nor will he be ordinary. He will be different. Get to know him, and you will notice something regal about him. And Jesus was different. When he came, he looked ordinary. But heaven pierced earth in a way it never had before, and people were amazed at him.

> The people were amazed at his teaching, because he taught them as one who had authority, not as the teachers of the law. (Mark 1:22)

For example, he didn't say, "As Rabbi so-and-so taught." He said, "Thus says the Lord," or, even more audaciously, "Verily, verily *I* say to you," which claimed great personal authority. The people listened. They knew immediately that he was different from any other prophet. The amazement continued. Jesus cast out demons as a way of telling those demons, "Your authority is now over. The kingdom of God has come and I am it" (Mark 1:25–27).

Then there is the story about a boat ride that met some very rough seas. Jesus was sleeping in the stern. Apparently there was a small armada of boats following him, and the storm was getting worse. Swamped boats and dead seamen were sure to follow. The disciples, freaked out by the severity of the storm, finally said, "Teacher, don't you care if we drown?" (Mark 4:38). Who knows what they were hoping Jesus would do. They certainly didn't expect him to do what he did. He got up and rebuked the wind and waves, "Quiet! Be still!" (v. 39). The sea listened and stopped its fury.

This was all very nice. No one drowned. No one was hurt. The disciples even learned a lesson about trusting in Jesus. But the disciples didn't act like everything was okay. After Jesus calmed the storm, the Bible says that they were "terrified." "Who is this?" they asked. "Even the wind and the waves obey him!" (v. 41).

It was a déjà vu moment. *This sounds familiar,* they had to be thinking. *When did I hear about something like this before? A word, and creation responds.* And then they remembered Genesis 1. They were in the boat with their Creator. It turns out that Jesus was the one who, in the Old Testament psalms, said to all his creation, "Be still, and know that I am God; I will be exalted among the nations, I will be exalted in the earth" (Psalm 46:10). The disciples were watching that psalm come to life right in front of them.

In the past, when people found themselves in the throne room of the King, they fell down as though they were dead. The disciples knew it was time to bow down. The Creator had broken into creation. Where human beings had messed things up, he was going to make things right. He was going to re-create his world, and the disciples were going to be part of it. You are going to be a part of it too.

The disciple John understood the connection between what Jesus was doing and what happened at the very beginning of time. As a result, he begins his story about Jesus with those momentous words from Genesis 1:1: "In the beginning" (John 1:1). John even echoes the first day of creation when God said, "Let there be light." But now he is telling us the deeper reality. Jesus created the light because he *was* the light.

In the beginning was the Word, and the Word was with God, and the Word was God. He was with God in the beginning. Through him all things were made; without him nothing was made that has been made. In him was life, and that life was the light of men. The light shines in the darkness, but the darkness has not understood it. (John 1:1–5)

Jesus was the Creator-King, and he was coming to recreate his world—his people—that so needed fixing. What difference does it make that Jesus is the Creator and created you and all things? It certainly makes him bigger than you once saw him, but what else specifically?

Keep watching him. The Gospel of Mark tells of him leaving a trail of amazed, mouths-wide-open people. That's what holy ones do. People were amazed when he cast demons into a group of pigs (5:20). They were amazed when he raised a little girl from the dead (5:42), demonstrated greater wisdom than the older leaders of the people (6:2), and walked on water (6:51). After a while, people were so accustomed to being amazed by him that they were amazed when they simply saw him (9:15). All Jesus had to do was show up and people were amazed. It wasn't because he was good looking—he wasn't. Nor was he wealthy, powerful (in the world's terms), or entertaining. It was because he was the Messiah—the King—and the amazing things they were witnessing were a small part of his inauguration ceremonies. Today, Jesus is still the King. His kingdom is growing, he is still amazing, and he invites you to be part of his kingdom expansion.

Do you believe that? It is unbelievable, in one sense, but you can't help but believe. This is God himself inviting you to know him. So believe. Even more, trust him. You believe that Columbus discovered America. But that doesn't really make any difference in your day-to-day life. When you believe *in* or trust *in* a person, it makes all the difference. What would you say is the difference between believing that something is true and believing *in* a person? Think about your current relationships as you answer.

Let's review. One important step in avoiding the worship of other people is to grow in knowing God's holiness. When you know that God is holy, you can no longer be indifferent or distant from him. He breaks into your everyday life, which is the only way you can be liberated from the craving to fit in and stand out.

Let's say that you just gave a speech before hundreds of your peers. No doubt you were nervous beforehand. Compare that with someone asking you to give the lesson for the three-year-old Sunday school class. I'm guessing you would not be too rattled. You just spoke in a major venue, so in contrast, a small group of three-year-olds is not very intimidating. That's how the knowledge of the Lord begins to cast out the fear of other people. When you have been to the court of the King and lived to tell about it, the court of human opinion is less frightening.

If there is one thing you can be sure about the Lord, it is that he makes himself known to those who want to know him. Pray that these stories will be holy and amazing to you so you can know him better. What else do you want to pray along those lines?

12

A Story of the Redeemer

He was a young man, single. No real home, no real family. He did have some friends, but their behavior might make you wonder if that's what they were. His friends rarely understood him, many left when they no longer got what they wanted from the relationship, and at his darkest time they scattered. This is a brief bio of Jesus. His story reveals that the Creator has come close. The King has left his throne and chosen to take on the hassles of life so there would be no doubt that he understands your life. He understands because he lived it.

I remember Kurt Cobain's immense popularity when he played with Nirvana. Why was he so popular and revered? He knew all about life in a broken home, with its shattered expectations and despair. People identified with him. In a similar way, though you might not identify with Jesus' perfection and power, you certainly can identify with the rejection he experienced by those who said they loved him. If you are familiar with rejection, big-time rejection, you will be amazed at his holy story.

Throughout history, God's people have made it a tradition to run from him. It is all very bizarre, especially when you consider that God is the source of every good thing and he loves his creatures. For some strange reason, human beings don't naturally like God. We have a habit of ignoring him and running from him. One picture the Lord uses to talk about this is marriage and adultery. He is the husband, we are the wife, and we spend our time trying to run away from our spouse. Given those conditions, how could he possibly pursue us?

> "Return, faithless people," declares the LORD, "for I am your husband. I will choose you—one from a town and two from a clan—and bring you to Zion." (Jeremiah 3:14)

It's almost embarrassing. It *is* embarrassing to passionately invite a wife (husband, friend, boyfriend, or girlfriend) back after taking such abuse! But that is what God does.

For this story to mean anything to you, you have to know this: you are the wife God is talking about. You are the wife who keeps leaving. Such a person typically doesn't think about how much she is hurting her rejected husband. She is just doing what she wants to do. That's us when we run from the Lord to other things. We don't see it as an outright rejection of God. We are just doing what we want to do. In other words, we may acknowledge that we do wrong things sometimes, but it is tougher to acknowledge that our wrong was very personal and against God. It doesn't *feel* like it is personal, but it is.

Now add to this picture. The One who invites you back is also the King. What you did was treason. You betrayed the King, consorted with the enemy, and made it all very public. Why would you do such a thing? There is something in you that wants to be a god—a king—to manage your world on your own. Maybe when you get older, married, and dull, you can show allegiance to Jesus Christ because there will be less to lose at that point in your life. But right now the world is just too attractive for that. *That* is personal, and against God. It's undeniable.

Time to stop for a moment. It is starting to sound nasty again, and we are not really *that* bad. Betrayal, treason—those are strong words. They sound exaggerated. What's the big deal, really? The goal here is not to feel bad. The goal is simply to see clearly. If we saw everything we needed to see, there would be no reason to have a Bible. But the Bible gives us 3-D glasses for the world around us and an X ray for our hearts. It takes us out of our semiblind state and helps us to see things the way they really are. So, treason? Consorting with the enemy? Let me see.

- I see resentment that I have toward . . . more people than I thought. *Who am I?* I am a god. *Who are other people?* They live to serve me. *Who is God?* Someone I hope will leave me alone so I can judge these people and feel good about it. When it comes to resentment, I want to be God.
- I see that I like to be served much more than I like to serve.
- I see that I can speak against some people behind their backs. I wouldn't want some of my conversations to be public. *Who am I?* The judge. *Who is God?* Not holy. He must be just like a human being who can't hear everything I say or think.
- I see that I want to be loved more than I want to love.

That is enough of my list for today. Lord, have mercy. Does this fit your experience? Don't forget, all these things can go on under the surface without you being aware, but make no mistake, you are doing these things.

As it turns out, we are worse than we think. Who are you? An idolater. An adulterer. A lover of yourself and your own agenda. Seeing all this accurately moves you toward amazement that God would love you and want you to love him. No normal human being would tolerate such things and come back for more. If God were going to reject you after you rejected him, there would be no reason to even think about these things. Why dwell on things that are miserable and hopeless? The reason you are looking at yourself with such openness and honesty is because God does not reject you.

How does God do it? How does he keep from rejecting those who reject him? Well, he is love. But there is much more going on too. Rebellion against the King cannot go unpunished. Otherwise the kingdom of God is without any justice at all. Even humans can't gloss over oppression and injustice when they see it. It wouldn't be loving! In order to show justice, God chose to bring a crushing blow to sin through one perfect person who would represent all those who trusted in him. Jesus was the one who received that blow. That's why he is called the sacrificial lamb. The lamb in the Hebrew system was sacrificed so we didn't have to be. God the Son became human. He became the servant who was crucified as the way to bring justice and show love.

It may seem odd that Jesus was the representative for all those who trusted in him, but it does make sense. Presidents sign treaties on behalf of nations. The queen of England isn't just the queen; she represents and embodies the British Commonwealth. When you are younger your parent stands in your place, signs all the legal documents, and accepts any debts you accrue. It is common for someone to represent another. What is uncommon is that the person who represented you is the Son of God. The Son took on the rejection that you deserved from God himself, along with the punishment and death that go with it. Jesus died in your place. He experienced the awful rejection from the Father that you deserved for your rejection of him.

Have you ever received an unusually generous gift? Once I was given a small sailboat. It wasn't the fastest or sleekest in the fleet, but it was a working sailboat, and it was great fun. Every time I saw it I was changed. It was impossible to just look at it and be indifferent. I had to respond. I always responded with thanks. Sometimes I responded by imitating the generosity of my friend and thinking of other people I could share it with. Extravagant gifts change you. Are you changed by what Jesus did? Are you thankful—every day—and does his gift to you make you want to act like him? Why? Why not?

Some people have said that faith is like a step into the unknown, as in, "You just have to have faith." But there is nothing unknown about it. Faith is all about choosing sides. Will you put your trust in yourself or will you trust in the reigning King Jesus? To whom will you give your allegiance?

Does it seem odd that all you are asked to do is trust Jesus? It's not really odd. When you trust him, you are saying, "I am with him. My allegiance is to him, and what happens to him happens to me." Watch *Braveheart* or other movies with influential heroes. The fate of the followers is in the hands of the leader. When you say that Jesus is your King, you are saying that your fate rests in his hands. In this case, you acknowledge to the Father that, indeed, you do deserve the same punishment meted out to all treasonous people, but your allegiances are now with Jesus. You trust in him. That's how something that happened two thousand years ago is relevant to you right now. When you trust him, you stand with him. The punishment that was intended for you was received by him. And there is never again a reason to fear judgment. That is how God can relentlessly pursue unholy people and rain love on them rather than judgment.

Here is the story Jesus told about the way God loves and pursues people who reject him as Father and King.

> Jesus [said,] "There was a man who had two sons. The younger one said to his father, 'Father, give me my share of the estate.' So he divided his property between them.
>
> "Not long after that, the younger son got together all he had, set off for a distant country and there squandered his wealth in wild living. After he had spent everything, there was a severe famine in that whole country, and he began to be in need. So he went and hired himself out to a citizen of that country, who sent him to his fields to feed pigs. He longed to fill his stomach with the pods that the pigs were eating, but no one gave him anything.

"When he came to his senses, he said, 'How many of my father's hired men have food to spare, and here I am starving to death! I will set out and go back to my father and say to him: Father, I have sinned against heaven and against you. I am no longer worthy to be called your son; make me like one of your hired men.' So he got up and went to his father.

"But while he was still a long way off, his father saw him and was filled with compassion for him; he ran to his son, threw his arms around him and kissed him.

"The son said to him, 'Father, I have sinned against heaven and against you. I am no longer worthy to be called your son.'

"But the father said to his servants, 'Quick! Bring the best robe and put it on him. Put a ring on his finger and sandals on his feet. Bring the fattened calf and kill it. Let's have a feast and celebrate. For this son of mine was dead and is alive again; he was lost and is found.'" (Luke 15:11–24)

The father *ran* to his son. That is the remarkable thing about this story. Try to keep your attention more on God than yourself. Sure, the son was a mess, but the father ran to accept him. Keep in mind that the father was a very important person. Important people don't run. Servants run, masters don't. To do so would be very undignified. But this father ran. This is holy behavior. It is hard to believe that your heavenly Father runs to you when you run away from him? You might believe that he accepts you back, but it's hard to believe he runs after you and throws his arms around you. Do you believe that God runs toward his children as they turn toward him? Can you explain why God would do such a thing?

Without the cross of Jesus Christ, none of this would be possible. Justice would come screaming down on every one of us. But your heavenly Father invites you to cast your lot with Jesus. That's what it means to trust him. What happened to him happened to you. As a result, love and mercy will follow you for the rest of eternity.

Any thoughts on how to respond to all this? You have to do something with such a story. When you are shown extravagant grace—when you are given a great gift—you can't just think, *That's nice.* "Thank you" works better, but it should be a boisterous "Thank you!" What is your response to this story? Has it gotten your attention?

If you can't think of anything, here is an idea. Say, "Yes, Lord, I trust you." Say it out loud. Anything else?

Do you see the connection with the fear of other's opinions? For example, let's say that you are embarrassed to be publicly associated with Jesus. But when you know that Jesus is truly extraordinary, you are strangely tempted to tell someone about him. You are learning how the fear of the Lord wipes out the fear of other people. It makes you want to know him better, and God is eager to satisfy that desire. Keep asking him for the very best. Ask him to show himself to you in such a way that you fear him above all else.

13

Deep Mysteries about the Redeemer

There is a theme that you can find in movies. The new girl in school isn't fitting in. One day it is her clothes, the next it is her hair, the next it is her klutziness in gym class. There is always some new way to criticize her. Then she captures the interest of the most popular guy in the school, or she is seen being picked up after school by some incredibly handsome rich guy and everything changes. When she has her eyes on this popular or mysterious new person, all is well. Apparently, a relationship is the answer.

You don't find the answer to paralyzing self-consciousness by giving yourself a pep talk about how great you are. All you have to do is get connected to the right person, and that is the path you are on. At first, learning about someone else as a way to deal with your own problems seems like an odd strategy. But that is how you change. Put your attention more on Jesus than yourself, and things begin to happen. It is worth pausing a little longer in order to consider who Jesus is and what he did.

Most people think that Jesus is a nice (though somewhat wimpy) example to follow. That will never do if you want to be less controlled by others. Connecting to a wimp won't help. You need the Holy One, who is big enough to give you a reason to live for him rather than yourself and the opinions of others. You need to know him as the reigning King. You need to know that his cross was the demonstration of power that changed all of human history.

With this in mind, consider another passage from the Bible. This is from the apostle Paul's letter to the Christians who lived in Rome. It is meatier than most other passages, so it takes a little more work, but it will remind you that Jesus did more than you think. We will pick up his letter with Paul telling us that Jesus did something amazing.

> You see, at just the right time, when we were still powerless, Christ died for the ungodly. Very rarely will anyone die for a righteous man, though for a good man someone might possibly dare to die. But God demonstrates his own love for us in this: While we were still sinners, Christ died for us. (Romans 5:6–8)

These three verses by themselves are enough to keep you busy for the next year.

Who are we, according to Paul?

Who is the Lord?

Put this passage into your own words.

What difference does this make?

- If Jesus already died for me, when I did not like him, I know he loves me now.

-

-

In the next section you encounter the word *justified*. This is a legal term that means both "not guilty" and "declared righteous." King Jesus has measured up to the requirements of God's commands on your behalf. If your allegiances are to him, you are given what is his. Notice that the two following verses say almost the same thing but with different imagery. The first image is the courtroom. The second is that of an enemy.

> Since we have now been justified by his [Jesus'] blood, how much more shall we be saved from God's wrath through him! For if, when we were God's enemies, we were reconciled to him through the death of his Son, how much more, having been reconciled, shall we be saved through his life! (Romans 5:9–10)

We too often think that there is nothing personal about our indifference toward and avoidance of Jesus Christ. Nothing against him; we just wanted to do what we wanted to do. But these verses spell out our treason. Who am I? Prone to insurrection and rebellion against the King, and guilty. Explain why this does or does not make sense to you.

What about the word *enemy*? Do you see how you were and can still act like God's enemy? Can you think of some concrete examples of this?

Yet—and this is very important—he didn't wait for you to shape up before he came to get you. Instead, he brought you back to himself, even while you were still acting like an enemy. No mere mortal would ever do such a thing. If you have declared that you are with King Jesus, this is a reason to be happy.

> Not only is this so, but we also rejoice in God through our Lord Jesus Christ, through whom we have now received reconciliation. (Romans 5:11)

Don't forget, the path you are on can show you hard things about yourself, but it also is a path of thankfulness and joy.

The next six verses repeat one theme: you were a child of Adam, and you were under the sentence of death because you were joined to him. Now by trusting Jesus you are identified with him and the benefits never stop.

You didn't realize that what Adam did affected you so much, but this too makes sense. What your parents do certainly affects you. If they are destitute, so are you. If they are born into a low social class in India, so are you. In a similar way, Adam represented you. When he sinned, he was your leader or representative. It might sound unfair that you are guilty because of what someone else did, until you keep reading and find that, by simply trusting in Jesus the King, you receive everything that was his. He has become your new representative. All you do is say, "I'm with him."

Therefore, just as sin entered the world through one man [Adam], and death through sin, and in this way death came to all men, because all sinned . . . But the gift [of Jesus] is not like the trespass. For if the many died by the trespass of the one man [Adam], how much more did God's grace and the gift that came by the grace of the one man, Jesus Christ, overflow to the many! Again, the gift of God is not like the result of the one man's sin: The judgment followed one sin and brought condemnation, but the gift followed many trespasses and brought justification. For if, by the trespass of the one man, death reigned through that one man, how much more will those who receive God's abundant provision of grace and of the gift of righteousness reign in life through the one man, Jesus Christ.

Consequently, just as the result of one trespass was condemnation for all men, so also the result of one act of righteousness was justification that brings life for all men. For just as through the disobedience of the one man the many were made sinners, so also through the obedience of the one man the many will be made righteous. (Romans 5:12, 15–19)

Try to put this into your own words. Keep in mind that we are trying to see everything bigger than we once did. The cross of Jesus was huge. It casts its shadow over everything that came after it. You are part of a family tree, and there is no escaping that. Is Adam your representative, or is Jesus? If you have decided that Jesus is your King, here is the way to respond: "Rejoice in God through our Lord Jesus Christ, through whom we have now received reconciliation." Are you able to thank God, and be happy because of what Jesus did? Go ahead and say it.

14

Worshiping the Holy One

Do you ever sing songs about Jesus that really get to you? If so, you are worshiping. You are being exactly who you were intended to be. When you worship—when your attention is on the One who is bigger than yourself, and his love connects you to himself—the cares of life are not so controlling. True worship puts everything in perspective. It makes some of your fears about people's opinions seem trivial. That experience, though it can be terribly brief for most of us, is what we want to prolong. You are on a journey to learn that God is really big and that he is holy. We want to know his holiness well enough that worship becomes natural. Are you getting the knack of it? Do you see the freedom true worship delivers? When have you truly worshiped?

Worship is about choosing sides and publicly stating our allegiances. God has determined that, when he ushers in his kingdom in all its brilliance, our allegiances will be all that matter. And these allegiances are all about Jesus. Jesus Christ is the center of everything. The mark of your allegiance will be your trust in him over yourself and your idols. This means that there will be no surprises for you when you see Jesus. You know whether he is your King or not. If you have confessed that he is your King and Lord, and you are forgiven because of his sacrifice on the cross, you have nothing to fear.

Are you perfect in your allegiances? Are you unswervingly loyal to the Lord? Of course not. One of the marks of God's people is their awareness that they are not perfect. There is no room for arrogance in the fear of the Lord. What God's people do, however, is turn back to him when they see that they are wandering away.

If your lifestyle makes you wonder if Jesus really is your King, that is actually a good thing. You are understanding the truth. But you should also be amazed that the King never stops inviting you to himself and his kingdom. That is either very weird, or it's holy. If someone kept offering you a free invitation to a grand and expensive party, and you kept shoving it back in his face, at some point the host would stop making the offer. But God loves to invite you. He loves to invite those who can't pay the cover charge, so that he can pay it for them. That way, you and everyone else know that God himself did it all. You added nothing to make the relationship possible. That is what people mean by grace. There is no room for boasting.

If you know God as Holy Father, King, and Lord, you are moving in a direction from astonishment to devotion, devotion to reverence, and reverence to worship that delights in obeying him. Here is an image taken from the first appearance of the word *holy* in Scripture. As Scripture progresses, you learn more and more about God's holiness, so this image gets revised, but it is still a good one.

> Now Moses was tending the flock of Jethro his father-in-law, the priest of Midian, and he led the flock to the far side of the desert and came to Horeb, the mountain of God. There the angel of the LORD appeared to him in flames of fire from within a bush. Moses saw that though the bush was on fire it did not

burn up. So Moses thought, "I will go over and see this strange sight—why the bush does not burn up."

When the LORD saw that he had gone over to look, God called to him from within the bush, "Moses! Moses!"

And Moses said, "Here I am."

"Do not come any closer," God said. "Take off your sandals, for the place where you are standing is *holy* ground." (Exodus 3:1–5, emphasis added)

Little did Moses realize that the God of the cosmos was also the God who comes very close. The burning bush was serving as his throne room, and Moses knew that when you come into the King's presence, you take off your shoes. It is a sign of respect. That is fear in the good sense of the word. That is a way you can worship the Lord. From this initial picture of God's holiness your goal is to *walk through life with your shoes off*. It means that you live *coram Deo*, a phrase meaning "before the face of God." God's throne room extends everywhere, so you always live with your shoes off.

Can you picture it? Everywhere you look there is a bush burning. God is present. The *big* God is present, and his presence puts everything in perspective. Those things that once seemed to be so important, such as the admiration, love, and respect of others, are no longer "burning" issues (sorry).

What a great class in the fear of the Lord for Moses! And he was going to need it. He was going to be squaring off with Pharaoh, and Pharaoh could make life and death decisions on a whim. Most people found Pharaoh very intimidating. But when you hang out in the throne room of God, earthly kings seem a good bit smaller. What would it mean for you to walk through life with your shoes off?

Can you imagine how this might affect the way you are controlled by the opinions of others?

It's hard to believe that the God of the universe comes close. In fact, there are times when you don't want him to come close. Either he scares you or you think he will tell you not to do things you want to do. But when you really get to know Jesus, you want him close, and you want to move toward him. He is too loving and beautiful to avoid. In the Gospel of Luke we meet a woman who understood this about Jesus. She is the first person in the New Testament to be called a woman of faith.

> As Jesus was on his way, the crowds almost crushed him. And a woman was there who had been subject to bleeding for twelve years, but no one could heal her. She came up behind him and touched the edge of his cloak, and immediately her bleeding stopped.
>
> "Who touched me?" Jesus asked.
>
> When they all denied it, Peter said, "Master, the people are crowding and pressing against you."
>
> But Jesus said, "Someone touched me; I know that power has gone out from me."
>
> Then the woman, seeing that she could not go unnoticed, came trembling and fell at his feet. In the presence of all the people, she told why she had touched him and how she had been instantly healed.
>
> Then he said to her, "Daughter, your faith has healed you. Go in peace." (Luke 8:42–48)

It's important to know that this woman was an outcast. In those days, anyone who was bleeding had to stay away from other people.

She wasn't allowed to touch others, and others weren't allowed to touch her. But she knew enough about Jesus to understand that those old rules were passing away. The real King had finally come. The Holy One who sat on the throne of the universe was coming very close, and he invited outcasts to touch him and be healed. The way she took her shoes off was by heeding Jesus' invitation to come to him.

If you feel like someone who never fits in, Jesus says, "Come." Who could refuse such an invitation? There are many different ways we can worship. Only one is by singing songs. Will you come to him?

Tania did. Her life was teetering on the brink of destruction, and she was only nineteen. Casual sex and drinking with friends, fueled by mounting hopelessness and isolation, were already becoming the identifying features of her life.

"Here is a place to start. Wise people know that this world is their Father's throne room, and they take their shoes off."

That wasn't the only thing someone said to her, but it marked the moment when she woke up. She was ready to hear this. So she took her shoes off. Since sex was driven by her desire for acceptance, that stopped quickly. Drinking too, for the same reason. The very concrete reminder that she lived in the presence of the loving King—her bare feet—assured her that she was not alone, and though she couldn't explain why, she noticed something she could identify as peace in her life.

Why? She had turned to the better Lord. The gods of acceptance and "Will you love me?" no longer governed her. In her case, it was the first time she turned. For others like her, it was the most recent about-face of hundreds of others.

The fear of the Lord—it means that you take your shoes off in his presence rather than wander off on a rocky and hazardous path. It means that you come. Tell the King who comes close to you that you are with him.

The Problem
The Heart of the Matter
Who Is God?

Who Am I?

Who Are They?

Who Am I?

It is tempting to stick with the question, who is God? You never completely leave it. But you need to add the other two questions. If you don't want to be stuck in the swamp of identity crises, insecurity, and self-loathing you need to answer—accurately and truly—the question, who am I? Otherwise, the amazing things about God will bounce off you rather than get all the way to your heart.

15

What Do I Need? What Should I Want?

"I can't live without him. I *need* him." Guys can say the same thing: "I can't live without *her.*" (But they usually *think* it rather than say it.) There it is: the cup, hoping to get filled with approval and affection, but constantly leaking. It's time for version 2.0 of yourself. Sure, the idea that you are a cup of needs that must be filled feels accurate. Everyone can relate to feeling empty and in dire need of affection and approval from the right person. But it all seems a little off too, doesn't it?

Okay, so who are you? What are alternatives to cups, idols, masks, and walls? Let's think about what you really need. Would you agree that sometimes you don't know what you need? Your body might be screaming for vitamin C and you give it a Mountain Dew. You think you need to relax to get your energy back, when a little exercise is the real answer. You think you need freedom, when what you need are clearer guardrails for a life that is careening out of control.

Since you can't always trust what you feel, one way to investigate what you really need is to examine some of the prayers in Scripture. Prayers are all about desperation and need. Find model prayers in Scripture, and you will find what you really need. The best place to start looking is the Lord's Prayer.

- Father, hallowed be your name.
- Your kingdom come.
- Give us each day our daily bread.
- Forgive us our sins, for we also forgive everyone who sins against us.
- And lead us not into temptation. (Luke 11:2–4)

There they are. Your deepest needs.

"Hallowed be your name"

The prayer starts the way most prayers in Scripture begin—with remembering who God is. No immediate launching into requests, as if you were sitting on Santa's lap. That isn't the way to talk to the King, even when he is your Father. So you begin by remembering and actually saying something about who he is.

If a good friend wants to ask for a favor or advice in a difficult situation, he or she might begin like this: "You are such a good friend. I value you and our relationship so much. When I realized I was struggling with something, you are the first person I thought of. I knew I could trust you." It would be odd to jump to the request without acknowledging any appreciation for the relationship. In a similar way, when you talk to the Lord, you can call him Father, which is loaded with hope. Also, you come to him with reverence. You "hallow" his name, which means that you speak to him with the keen awareness that he is the Holy God and you are not. You need your Father to be respected and known as great. You might as well pray that now.

"Your kingdom come"

When you ask for his kingdom to come you are asking that the royal reign that began with Jesus' resurrection would grow and break into the nations, your local community, and your own heart with justice, unity, and love. The kingdom is on the move, and you are praying that it would continue.

When you have a few minutes to pray, touch on each area—global, local, and personal. You need them all. You need the warring nations to come to Christ; you need injustice around the world to cease; you need your church, your family, and your friends to grow in humility, faith, and love; and you need a heart that is more and more devoted to your King and him alone.

"Give us each day our daily bread"

Daily physical needs? God created the real world and knows that you have physical needs for food, safety, health, and shelter. He invites you to ask for those needs, but you should add a request for grace to accept his provision, especially when you always want more than you have.

"Forgive us our sins, for we also forgive everyone who sins against us"

Then you come to your spiritual needs. According to this prayer, your greatest problem is your sin. That problem has priority over everything else because it has eternal significance. Other problems—hurts in relationships, or not meeting your goals in school or work—will stop at some point. But if you are not forgiven, your problems never end. So you pray for daily forgiveness, and your Father is delighted to forgive you.

Then, if you have been shown mercy and grace, you show the same thing to others. Jesus told a story about a man who had been forgiven a debt of millions of dollars and then immediately went out and threatened someone who owed him some spare change (Matthew 18:21–35). That is a gross injustice.

It works the same way with forgiveness. If you know you have been forgiven, you will forgive and reconcile with others. If you don't, you must believe that your sins were not that bad compared to the person you are judging. So another of your deepest needs is to forgive and reconcile with others.

"And lead us not into temptation"

There is one other request. "Lead us not into temptation," which can be understood as "give me spiritual strength so I don't give in to temptation." You live in a spiritual war zone, and there is a battle for your allegiances every hour. With this in mind, you need wisdom and power to know how to reaffirm your allegiances to the true God. Or you could pray the same thing another way: "Lord, teach me to worship you by delighting in obedience, especially when I want one thing and you say another."

There they are. Those are your basic needs. Like everything else in life, our needs must be interpreted through the lens of the Bible. If we saw everything clearly, there would be no reason for God to say anything else. It would be redundant. But everything is blotchy shades of gray unless God teaches us how to see. We don't always know what we need.

This should come as no surprise. Don't forget, when it comes to the physical body, most people would prefer a steady diet of Mountain Dew, cheese fries, donuts, and popcorn with extra butter—if they just ate what they thought they needed. Your sense of need doesn't always tell the truth. So your goal is still to really listen to God, which means listen and do something. Talk about this prayer with others who follow Jesus the King. Break it into sections and personalize it. And, of course, pray it.

Here is another way to get at what we need. Assume that Scripture is showing us how to be real human beings. If that's the case, then every command in Scripture is what we need. What commands of God are especially hard for you?

Can you think of a time when obeying God's command might have been hard but made you feel good?

You can get there, though it might take a few years. All those commands are summed up this way: love God and love your neighbor (Matthew 7:12; 22:34–40). These are your deep needs. Welcome to the mysteries of the universe revealed.

16

Love More Than Need

We like our relationships symmetrical. If I like you, I want you to like me back. Actually, that isn't quite true. If I like you, I want you to like me back a little more than I like you. We prefer to be liked, loved, admired more than we want to like, love, or admire. That imbalance gives power in a relationship, and by power I mean the less invested person has less chance of being hurt. So goes the arithmetic of human relationships until Jesus shows how things are supposed to be.

If you want to know more about yourself, turn to Jesus. When you look at him, you see the way you were intended to be. No, you weren't intended to raise the dead and turn water into wine, but you were created in the image of God, and Jesus is *the* image. Watch him to see how life in the kingdom of God really works.

One of the first things you notice about Jesus is that his earthly life was one rejection and abandonment after another (Mark 14). If anyone should have felt empty and needy for acceptance, it was Jesus. Yet the insults and betrayals didn't destroy him. How did he do it? His secret was simple. He loved the praise of God more than the praise of people. His desire was to love the Father and do the Father's will more than it was to receive the affection of others. That was key for him.

Jesus loved people more than he wanted to be loved by people. Jesus needed to love people more than he needed love from them.

For you, this means that true freedom in your relationships comes when the scales are always a little unbalanced: You want the weight to be more on the "love" side than the "be loved" side.

Plumb the depths of your humanity and you find that life is about love, but it is a more sophisticated kind of love than what the world portrays. "I really love her. I feel so good when I am with her." That's not exactly a deep definition of love. It is more interested in getting than giving. Whoever fills you the best is the one you'll love. No wonder there is so much divorce; that kind of love will only last forty-five minutes in the real world.

Go to school and at some point you will feel painfully self-conscious. It might be because your complexion is bad, or you failed publicly at something, or you overheard a criticism about yourself—even though it was no different from what you have said about other people. Still, it hurt big time. Now imagine having your universe put right side up. You are no longer the center. You remember that you are created to live for God, not yourself. He has pursued you to the ends of the earth to make you his own. So you set out on your mission of loving other people.

Can you see it? No more masks and painful insecurity. Instead, you are looking to bless, know, build up, ask forgiveness from, and reconcile with others. You might even speak out and ask why someone is being so mean. In doing these things, you are more interested in loving others than in being loved in return. You have such a full job description that you have less time to dwell on what other people might be thinking. You are a force of nature, an unstoppable love offensive. Nothing and nobody can get in your way. The one who loves more is the one with the power.

Does it still hurt to be left out, judged, or ignored? Absolutely. It hurts, but it doesn't control you. It doesn't eat away at the core of your being. Does this mean you have to swallow your pain without talking to the person who hurt you? No way. There are thousands of ways that love can be expressed. They range from being angry against injustice and confronting the person who did it, to overlooking the offense and looking to bless instead of curse. Do you notice the sting of rejection in any of your relationships? What do you do with that hurt?

Can you imagine what love (love you give) would look like in that relationship?

One relationship that can be difficult is the one with your parents. It is easy to get frustrated with a parent when you feel that you aren't being treated well. If life is all about your wants and desires, you will just stay frustrated until (a) you get what you want, or (b) the matter blows over and some other frustrating thing takes its place. But if you take the form of a servant who has been loved by God and now owes love to others (Romans 13:8), you can actually bridge the chasm between yourself and the other person. You might not know exactly what to say, but you do know that love moves toward other people rather than away from them. You also know that love takes the path of humility instead of arrogant judgment.

This is a tall order, no question about it. You are going to have to go back to Jesus the King over and over. That's where you get the power to do the impossible. When Paul experienced problems in his relationships, he boiled the truth down to this simple teaching: Christ and him crucified (1 Corinthians 2:2). That said it all, and it helped Paul get his life in perspective. Jesus Christ chose a shameful death on the cross so you wouldn't have to. He came to be the servant who followed the path of sacrificial love. If this is how the King served you, then you can serve others with his power.

> This is love: not that we loved God, but that he loved us and sent his Son as an atoning sacrifice for our sins. Dear friends, since God so loved us, we also ought to love one another. No one has ever seen God; but if we love one another, God lives in us and his love is made complete in us. We know that we live in him and he in us, because he has given us of his Spirit . . . We love because he first loved us. (1 John 4:10–13, 19)

There is only one way you could want to love others more than they love you: realizing that you have been loved more than you could ever love in return. Then everything begins to make sense. Your goal is to have a slight imbalance between loving and being loved. You want more weight on the loving side, even if it is a gram or two.

Who are you? Someone who was an enemy but was shown love. Now you get the opportunity to do that with others. Yes, it is hard, but it should also feel like that dolphin riding a wave. You have an opportunity to be an authentic human. Think practically about this one. What would it look like to love this way in real life?

- When I have been hurt in a relationship, I won't just ignore the problem. I will at least pray that God would give me his Spirit to both understand and do his will.
- I could ask a pastor, parent, or older wise person to pray for me and even give me advice.
- I could show kindness to the other person.
- I could not complain about the person to other people.
- I could remember that what was done to me is no different from what I do to others, even if what I do is only in my own imagination.
- I could pray for the person who has hurt me.

Who am I? Beloved by God. He loved me more than I love him, and now I get to love other people more than they love me. Who am I? You have heard the name "Christian" before. It simply means that you trust in Jesus rather than yourself. You follow him. Well, if that fits you, you are a Christian.

When women marry, they often change their last name to that of their husband. Keep that image in mind when you call yourself a Christian. Your name is Paul Christian, Sarah Christian, Jaden Christian, Natasha Christian. Every time you remember your last name, you realize that you are not a solitary, independent person. You are always connected to the One with whom you share a name. Furthermore, you don't just represent yourself, but you represent the other person. You are an ambassador. You speak on his behalf. You live with that other person in mind.

Try going through the next few days substituting "Christian" for your last name. You don't have to write it on papers, but that doesn't make this a pretend assignment. If you belong to Jesus, you really do take his name, and you are learning that there is power and freedom in wanting to love more than wanting to be loved.

17

It's Not about Me

When summer comes, the world heads for the beach. It's cooler. If you aren't preoccupied with sharks and other sea creatures, there are fun things to do in the surf. Tans are hard on the skin, but people tend to look nice with a healthy glow. Everyone likes the beach.

But there is more to it than waves and tans. What is it about a huge expanse of water that is relaxing and enjoyable? One thing people do at the beach is simply look at the ocean for hours. Only those who are absolutely committed to tanning turn their towels away to face the sun. The rest always want to keep an eye on the water. The same thing happens whenever you see something really huge, like the Grand Canyon, the Rocky Mountains, or just a big sky. It feels right and good when you are in the presence of something bigger than yourself. That is what you are aiming for.

Who am I? A balloon-boy or -girl who needs to puff myself up so I can feel better about myself. You thought that large helpings of self-esteem would make you feel better about yourself, so that the opinions of others wouldn't be so controlling. But almost the opposite is true. What you really need is to be with something so big that you can think less often about yourself. If you identify yourself as a Christian, you are beginning to understand that. In other words, the problem is that people are too big, you and your desires are even bigger, and God is too small. The problem at its very root is answered in being connected to Jesus. Who are we really?

- We are all small, and God is big.
- We are royal children who represent the King.
- We are Christians who live to make Jesus famous.
- We are humble servants who take our shoes off.
- We are loved, so we love.
- We are part of a nation on a mission, sent by our Father.
- We are true worshipers.

All these identities depend on knowing that God is big and holy. We get into trouble when we act like God is a genie whose lamp we rub when things are really hard, or a nice grandfatherly chap who pats us on the head and sneaks a dollar bill into our hand. The reality is that the Creator-God entered this world in the middle of history and made Jesus Christ the King ("Christ" is the same thing as "King"). Now he is gradually gathering the nations—and individuals like you—to himself, as a prelude to the time when all people will bow down to him as the rightful King of kings. "'As surely as I live,' says the Lord, 'every knee will bow before me; every tongue will confess to God'" (Romans 14:11). Does that sound big? And, just as importantly, does it sound good? Why, or why not?

Do you believe that someday the world will see that Jesus alone is the true King? Catch a glimpse of it. King Jesus is the only one big enough to capture your attention in such a way that you will think less often about yourself. It's true; life isn't about you! Yes, that's a shocker. Throughout history, the goal of every one of us human beings has instinctively been to establish our own personal greatness, even if it meant being the worst at something. "Puffed up" is what the apostle Paul called it. But that is not the way we were intended to live. The best way to live—the way you will be most happy—is to make life more about God and other people than it is about you. Can you imagine the benefit of thinking less frequently about yourself? How might it affect your daily life?

You've already heard the word *glory*. On Christmas, you hear about angels singing "glory to God in the highest." When something is glorious, it is unmistakably beautiful. You don't keep glory hidden. When someone wants all the glory, it means that he wants to be front and center. He wants to be the one who reaps the fame. We all want glory. But glory belongs to God. He is the one who should be seen.

The heavens declare the glory of God; the skies proclaim the work of his hands. (Psalm 19:1)

In his temple all cry, "Glory!" (Psalm 29:9)

Be exalted, O God, above the heavens; let your glory be over all the earth. (Psalm 57:5)

"Holy, holy, holy is the Lord Almighty; the whole earth is full of his glory." (Isaiah 6:3)

The Word became flesh and made his dwelling among us. We have seen his glory, the glory of the One and Only, who came from the Father, full of grace and truth. (John 1:14)

When God says that we should do everything for his glory (1 Corinthians 10:31), he is saying that our lives are intended to make him famous, not ourselves. If you read the first chapter of Ephesians you will read, over and over, that we are intended to live "to the praise of his glory." This means that you will actually enjoy giving glory to God. You were created to do such things. It is better than waking up with a seat overlooking the Grand Canyon. It is better than being on a Hawaiian beach with your best friends, watching waves the size of skyscrapers.

How do you do it? Start by praying. First, that you would know him and his love. Second, that you would love others in a way that would increase his fame. Then think in terms of small steps of love. Keep in step with what the Spirit is doing. You might not know the entire path in front of you. Just take that next step. Of course, you will still feel hurt when you are rejected. You will have a case of the blues when you fail at something important to you. These things are important to the Lord, and they will hurt, but these hurts won't be as lethal. At one time they might have put you in complete despair, even to the point where you think life isn't worth living. Now you might not go so low or for so long. Instead, you will be able to tell God about your hurts, ask him for comfort, and then think about how to live for him with your shoes off. What hurts and failures do you want to bring to the Lord? Speak them to him.

Since he is your Father, he promises to comfort you.

Praise be to the God and Father of our Lord Jesus Christ, the Father of compassion and the God of all comfort, who comforts us in all our troubles, so that we can comfort those in any trouble with the comfort we ourselves have received from

God. For just as the sufferings of Christ flow over into our lives, so also through Christ our comfort overflows. (2 Corinthians 1:3–5)

"I have seen his ways, but I will heal him; I will guide him and restore comfort to him, creating praise on the lips of the mourners in Israel. Peace, peace, to those far and near," says the LORD. "And I will heal them." (Isaiah 57:18–19)

You can pray for this comfort. Better yet, since it is a promise that God makes to you, look for it. It might not come in the ways you expected, but it will come. Can you think of times when you were in a dark place and God broke through with comfort? It could have been through the words of a friend.

Now you have a mission. You are a child of the King. Your Father is doing big things in his kingdom and you are part of it. What is your mission right now? List some of the possibilities below. What you are looking for are small steps of obedience—maybe even joyful obedience—that are a much bigger deal than you think. The King has determined that his kingdom will advance by means of these small steps.

- Call a friend and say how thankful you are for him or her.
- Ask for someone's forgiveness.
- Serve around the house.
- Do homework.
- Take out your Bible and read one story that is mentioned in this book.
- Ask a friend to pray for you.

- Ask a parent to pray for you.
- Greet someone others neglect.

-

-

-

When we set off to live for the glory of King Jesus, our mission might not look very spectacular. No mission trips around the world. No Jesus decals on your books that bring thousands to the Truth. Jesus did everyday things, and when he did, the ordinary work of life became extraordinary. In other words, if you want to do something very spiritual, live for the King by picking up your room or doing the thing that is right in front of you. As you do, you will also notice that you are thinking less often about the possible opinions of other people.

The Problem
The Heart of the Matter
Who Is God?
Who Am I?

Who Are They?

Who Are *They?*

Two questions down, one to go, although you never leave those first two questions behind completely. Having looked at who God is, you revised the picture of yourself. Now you can look at other people accurately. Friends or enemies, you can be certain that they are all people you can love. Your being human depends on it.

18

Enemies + Friends + Loved Ones = Family

We all have our ways of cataloging people: jocks, jerks, nerds, even vampires. The possibilities are endless. When you read the Bible you will notice people who are enemies, acquaintances, friends, and loved ones. They don't always stay in the same group—enemies can become friends, loved ones can become enemies—but everyone fits into at least one.

Yet there is one category that God uses for all of these people: family. Here is a story Jesus told a religious leader who tried to test him. The man was a Jew. The hero of the story, much to the chagrin of this religious leader, was a Samaritan. As you might know, Jews never associated with Samaritans and considered them inferior.

On one occasion an expert in the law stood up to test Jesus. "Teacher," he asked, "what must I do to inherit eternal life?"

"What is written in the Law?" he replied. "How do you read it?"

He answered: "'Love the Lord your God with all your heart and with all your soul and with all your strength and with all your mind'; and, 'Love your neighbor as yourself.'"

"You have answered correctly," Jesus replied. "Do this and you will live."

But he wanted to justify himself, so he asked Jesus, "And who is my neighbor?"

In reply Jesus said: "A man was going down from Jerusalem to Jericho, when he fell into the hands of robbers. They stripped him of his clothes, beat him and went away, leaving him half dead. A priest happened to be going down the same road, and when he saw the man, he passed by on the other side. So too, a Levite, when he came to the place and saw him, passed by on the other side. But a Samaritan, as he traveled, came where the man was; and when he saw him, he took pity on him. He went to him and bandaged his wounds, pouring on oil and wine. Then he put the man on his own donkey, took him to an inn and took care of him. The next day he took out two silver coins and gave them to the innkeeper. 'Look after him,' he said, 'and when I return, I will reimburse you for any extra expense you may have.'

"Which of these three do you think was a neighbor to the man who fell into the hands of robbers?"

The expert in the law replied, "The one who had mercy on him."

Jesus told him, "Go and do likewise." (Luke 10:25–37)

Most of the people in your life are neighbors, a group that blends acquaintances and friends. They go to school with you, they live within a ten-mile radius of your home, and they work in the local stores. You don't really think about most of them; you just notice that they are around. You might help a little old lady across the street every now and then, but for the most part, neighbors keep to themselves and take care of themselves.

Jesus is always happy to blow up your normal way of seeing the world. In this case he does it by saying that your enemies are neighbors, and your neighbors are family. What this Samaritan did for the half-dead Jewish man is what someone would have done for a son or a daughter, a brother or a sister, but not for an enemy. The Samaritan goes out of his way to help; money is no object. No doubt, this exceeds what many people do for their own flesh and blood.

Now imagine for a moment. What would happen to your self-consciousness if you treated everyone as family? Usually, when you are home with family, you don't spend too much time thinking about their opinions of you. You aren't worried about your hair, weight, successes, or failures. They might drive you crazy sometimes, but you deal with it. You have to. They are family. This sense of family might even extend to your very good friends. When you are with them, you aren't as focused on yourself. People who are shy at school can be chatterboxes at home. You wear whatever you want in the house; it's the moment you walk out the door that you suddenly get hit with the desire to be cool. The clothes that were fine a second before are now hideous.

Here is part of the deep wisdom of God's Word. God is the Creator—the Father of everyone, whether people acknowledge him or not. *Other people are family.* If they are human beings they have met the basic qualification, and we are called by God to love them like family. Think of a family time when you had no self-consciousness. Or think about a time with a good friend where you briefly forgot about yourself. What was it like?

Can you imagine life lived at all times in that same way? What would it be like?

Here is the challenge. It goes back to loving others more than needing them. There is something about love that crowds out our painful self-consciousness. You can't have one in your heart when the other is there. Consider the needs of others more than you consider your own, and guaranteed, the fear of other people will no longer suffocate you.

It's time to expand the boundaries of your immediate family so that they include your neighbors, which means everyone. Can you think of practical ways to do that? Make a list of the different people you meet every day. Think about how you can include them as family. What will you actually do? How will you greet them? What will you talk to them about? What kinds of questions will you ask them? And how will you pray?

19

"No, *You* Are More Worthy"

Two young girls were playing grown-up at the front door of a fancy hotel.

"After you," one said with a British accent, or at least a hoity-toity one.

"No, after you."

"No, after you, I insist." She sounded like Julia Child. After a few more rounds the giggles got the better of them. Who knows who they were imitating? I never actually observed such deference in real life, but it was sweet and funny, and they were demonstrating exactly what we are aiming for.

We want to think more about the good of others and less often about our own good. Yes, it might take a lifetime to get the knack of it, but it will be great fun working on it.

So keep in mind your goal: to love more than you need love. Who are other people? Family—objects of your affection.

Here is something from the apostle Paul again. As you would expect, the verses start with what Jesus has already done for you. That is always Paul's strategy. Before he calls you to do anything, he tells you what Jesus has already done. Jesus always goes first.

If you have any encouragement from being united with Christ, if any comfort from his love, if any fellowship with the Spirit, if any tenderness and compassion, then make my joy complete by being like-minded, having the same love, being one in spirit and purpose. (Philippians 2:1–2)

He is saying, "*If* you have any encouragement...," but he is really saying, "I *know* you have found great encouragement in what Jesus Christ has done for you. He has actually joined you with himself—what is his is yours—and you didn't have to earn it." This means that you don't necessarily do good deeds for Jesus; you do them *because* of Jesus. He always makes the first move; you simply respond out of gratitude. Next Paul tells you how to be a true human being.

Do nothing out of selfish ambition or vain conceit, but in humility consider others better than yourselves. Each of you should look not only to your own interests, but also to the interests of others. (Philippians 2:3–4)

At first it sounds like the Bible is saying that other people are more important than you are, which doesn't sound very good. But when you think about the rest of Scripture, you know that God emphasizes how we are all royalty. So what the apostle Paul is saying is that followers of Jesus Christ should live in humility and consider other people as worthy of preferential treatment. In other words, live as though it is everyone else's birthday. That's not a problem with a special friend one day a year, but to live that way with everyone? It's no wonder Paul keeps pointing you to Jesus Christ as the example, the motivation, and the power for this seemingly impossible task.

Your attitude should be the same as that of Christ Jesus: Who, being in very nature God, did not consider equality with God something to be grasped, but made himself nothing, taking the very nature of a servant, being made in human likeness. And being found in appearance as a man, he humbled himself and became obedient to death—even death on a cross!

Therefore God exalted him to the highest place and gave him the name that is above every name, that at the name of Jesus every knee should bow, in heaven and on earth and under the earth, and every tongue confess that Jesus Christ is Lord, to the glory of God the Father. (Philippians 2:5–11)

All eyes on Jesus. That is the way of change. Follow him and you learn that the way up is the way down.

Who am I? A kneeler before God. Someone who walks with my shoes off. Once we learn to walk humbly before the Lord, we find that the skill actually transfers to our relationships with other people. It is the way humans are intended to live. Who am I? Someone who has been given preferential treatment by the King himself. When you know that, it becomes a small thing to put others before yourself.

Jesus Christ considered your interests above his own, so you will want to do the same thing with others. Jesus Christ served you, so you will want to serve others. And somehow, you are elevated and feel more alive when you do such things. You are learning how to be the way you were created to be. How would you explain these verses to someone else?

Notice anything? Notice any winds of change in your own heart? If so, describe what's happening.

You treat others the way you have been treated. If your hero—your Lord and your God—made himself lower than other people, then it is your honor and privilege to do the same thing. One of the last things

Jesus did before he was crucified was to serve his disciples by washing their feet—something only servants did.

> "Do you understand what I have done for you?" he asked them. "You call me 'Teacher' and 'Lord,' and rightly so, for that is what I am. Now that I, your Lord and Teacher, have washed your feet, you also should wash one another's feet. I have set you an example that you should do as I have done for you. I tell you the truth, no servant is greater than his master, nor is a messenger greater than the one who sent him. Now that you know these things, you will be blessed if you do them." (John 13:12–17)

The way up is the way down—there it is again. When you look for spiritual direction, the compass is always pointing down. At first, it might not sound that great. But you know that the path down is good and satisfying because God has revealed mysteries to you about what it means to be a true human being. Did you ever have a fight about who would be first?

> "I want you to go first."
> "No, you."
> "No, you. You are more worthy."

Try to get the rhythm of change.

1. You start by looking at who God is and what he has done for you.
2. Then, in response, treat others the way you have been treated. Love more than you need love from other people.
3. Then get your eyes right back onto Jesus.

This has always been the path of change. You can even find it in the Ten Commandments. Those commandments don't actually begin with what we are supposed to do. Instead, they begin with God: "I am the Lord your God, who brought you out of Egypt, out of the land of slavery" (Exodus 20:2). If you were a slave who had just been freed, you would be all ears after hearing such an introduction. You would be eager to do whatever the Lord said. It makes you want to go out and love, doesn't it?

Final Thoughts

20

Companions on a Bumpy Road

Other people have taken this path before you. Yes, they could be intimidated by other people, but they also knew how to not be dominated by what others thought or did. Their goal wasn't to fit in or stand out. For them, life was more simple: they belonged to another, and they lived for him. They can be helpful guides.

In the Old Testament, Daniel, Shadrach, Meshach, and Abednego led the way for you (Daniel 3). If you had the choice between bowing down to a gold image of King Nebuchadnezzar or being thrown into a blazing furnace, chances are you would think twice. You could always bow down to the king, and in your own mind say that you were *respecting* him rather than worshiping him. Or you could keep your fingers crossed while you were on your knees. It is very easy to justify idolatry, especially when your life is on the line.

But the fear of the Lord simplifies life. For Shadrach, Meshach, and Abednego, the decision was easy. False worship or the furnace? The furnace it is. No hesitation. They knew that God *could* deliver them if he chose, though they had no reason to expect it. They had never witnessed God deliver someone from fire. But it didn't matter. It was simple: they would not worship a false image.

You probably know the story—they were delivered. God was with them in the furnace. But their deliverance isn't the point. What is amazing is that, despite having good reason to be controlled by other people, they chose to fear God. How did they do it?

Who were they? Who was God to them? Who were those other people?

In the New Testament, the apostle Paul stands out. Just take what happened when he went to tell the people in Corinth about Jesus the King. The people there had very clear expectations of what a teacher-guru should be. He should be a marvelous orator, be supported by rich patrons, and have an entourage. Paul could have been all these things, but he knew that if he was, he would be diluting the message of Christ by making it more about himself and his status than Jesus. So he purposely went against everything that could give him status and prestige. He used the simple language of the common people, refused patronage, and insisted that people follow Jesus, not him.

The Corinthian response was mixed. Some liked him, but most doubted whether someone so unimportant could speak on God's behalf. At one point they even asked him for a letter of reference, and this was after he had spent months with them. The Corinthians had withheld their affections. They didn't love Paul very much. His cup was, to be sure, close to empty. Their coolness hurt him deeply, but it didn't cause him to love them less. If you read 1 and 2 Corinthians you will find a man who always had the love and forgiveness of Jesus Christ in view. As a result, he took the initiative in love. He said, "I love you" before they said it to him.

> We have spoken freely to you, Corinthians, and opened wide our hearts to you. We are not withholding our affection from you, but you are withholding yours from us. As a fair exchange—I speak as to my children—open wide your hearts also. (2 Corinthians 6:11–13)

Who is Jesus? My Lord. I belong to him. He bought me at a great
price.
Who am I? I owe people. As I have been shown love that I could
never repay, I owe love to others.
Who are others? Brothers and sisters.

These men are on the short list of relatively famous people who
weren't controlled by the opinions of others. They are your compan-
ions. Yes, the list is short because, if you follow any current media,
film, or TV star, you will definitely find that the fear of man is driving
them. If you know your rock bands and movie stars, the honest ones
will always mention their grave self-doubt. They dread possible rejection by their fans, and they feel ill at ease with the outrageous success
that is theirs. Yet you can still find people who follow in the steps
of the three Hebrew men who were thrown into the flames, and the
apostle who loved people but was rejected by many.

When you get to know the ways of God, you find that he prefers to
do his greatest work in very ordinary people. If he showered his greatest glory on the wealthy and the wise, onlookers could just attribute
their success to their money and intelligence. Instead, God specializes
in people like you. Here are some of the ordinary people who have
done extraordinary things.

- A high-school girl wanted desperately to go to a party at a
  friend's house, but her parents said no. Instead of worrying
  that people would make fun of her for not going, she quietly
  accepted her parent's decision—after she made a brief but
  respectful appeal—and that was the end of it.
- A high-school boy who once loathed the process of finding a
  place to sit at lunch began to use it as a time to move toward
  people who seemed to be isolated.
- A youth group felt comfortable around each other because
  they considered each other as family.

- A girl had a friend whose parents bought her a very popular and expensive brand of shoes. This girl always liked those shoes, but never had the money to get them. When she saw that her friend was wearing the shoes she liked so much, she was genuinely happy for her friend.
- A nineteen-year-old guy decided to talk to his friends about the way they were treating another person in their group. This other person was, without question, difficult and egocentric, but the nineteen-year-old was convicted that the group was not loving this other person, so he told them, while acknowledging that he hadn't loved well either.
- A college student who had been secretly anorexic asked for help. Apart from Jesus, she would have been too ashamed to say anything.
- A guy asked a girl out and she refused, but he continued to care for her as a friend. He didn't even feel that awkward around her.
- A guy acknowledged to some friends that he went to church and liked it.
- A twenty-year-old chose not to contribute to conversations that veered off into gossip.
- A good friend said something hurtful, and rather than be crushed or bitter, the person who was hurt went and talked to the friend.
- A college student who struggled with depression started getting out of bed earlier because she had a mission: to love others as she had been loved.
- A college student reached out to a fellow student who was a neglected loner.

Who could you add to the list?

And you? You are seeking to worship God more than the opinions of others? Do you want to love people even if they don't love you as you would like? Not many people see what is happening in your heart, but if you made it this far, something is happening. When the Spirit changes you, there usually aren't bombs going off, and you have as many bad days as you have good. But you notice that you are turning to Jesus more. Then, as Jesus gets bigger in your eyes, the opinions of other people simply become . . . the opinions of other people and not the piercing gaze of giants. Your questions change from, "How can I protect myself, fit in, and look good?" to, "How can I wisely love another person?"

One of the great features of the way God created you is that you are always growing and changing. In fact, God will change you in noticeable ways and other people will see it. That is one way you can bring glory to him. So be bold, and ask him to keep changing you in noticeable ways.

> Be diligent in these matters; give yourself wholly to them, so that everyone may see your progress. (1 Timothy 4:15)

What is the next step of change for you? How do you want to pray to get started?

Welcome to the path of becoming truly human, where you are controlled by God more than other people, and where you love others more than need them to love you. It is hard, but it is wonderful. You're going to love it.

Scripture Index